INTO THE BLIZZARD

The Adventures of Jack Zachary,
"Heretic" of the Northland

By
Olivine Nadeau Bohner
(As told to her by J. H. Zachary, Sr.)

TEACH Services, Inc.
www.TEACHServices.com

Copyright © 2009 TEACH Services, Inc.
ISBN-13: 978-1-57258-158-6
Library of Congress Control Number: 99-68252

Published by
TEACH Services, Inc.
www.TEACHServices.com

Table of Contents

1

The First Faint Cry

Jacob Zachary always remembered the time that winter when he was three. He'd heard a strange sound in the thatch above the clay oven, and looking up, he saw flames around the chimney. Someone shouted, "Fire!" Jacob jumped from the bunk bed where he had been sitting and began to search for his shoes, under the bunks, the wooden benches, the homemade table. His mother hurried past him, shouting that she must loosen the cow tied in the lean-to. When she came back, the ceiling was ablaze. Jacob remembered her grabbing up the baby from her swinging willow basket. He remembered her throwing a blanket over him, and half dragging, half carrying him from the house, and dropping him into a snowbank.

The prickly cold made him cry. But after a while he stopped crying, hearing the excited voices of his father and his brothers, Charlie, John, and Alex, and the neighbor, Mike Bilyuk. They were shouting to each other as they carried pieces of furniture from the burning straw-thatched cabin. Fascinated, Jacob tried to watch them dodging in and out.

But the coldness soon numbed the little fellow so that the men and voices, and the crackling of the fire blurred. Then as if from afar off he heard his mother:

"Oh, my baby! My baby boy is dead! He's frozen white!"

Jacob felt himself being lifted in strong arms. He knew no more until he felt the stinging cold of icy water. He gasped for breath. They had plunged him, blanket and all, into a tub of water and snow. Then he heard his mother again, and the words came to him often through the years.

"Nothing must happen to this child. He has been dedicated to a holy mission."

Later, dried and wrapped warmly, Jacob lay on one of the neighbor's bunk beds watching his mother nearby nursing the baby, the three older boys and all the family possessions crowded around her. He noticed a tear slip down his mother's cheek and fall on the baby's soft hair.

The child could not know the hardships the family had had setting up a new home in Manitoba, Canada, at the turn of the century. The Zacharys had come with several families from the Ukraine. They had traveled from Winnipeg, the end of the railroad line, over mere trails skirting the bogs to take up homesteads fifty miles farther on. Helyar and Vasilenna Zachary had worked side by side building the log cabin. They thatched it with bulrushes. They built a clay oven to warm the cabin and to bake in. Vasilenna wove willow wands to make bunk beds for her family.

The second summer they added a lean-to in which to keep the cow and a root cellar in which to store the vegetables produced so abundantly that year in the rich soil.

When the grain crop ripened, they cut it, bound it into sheaves, and stored the sheaves under piles of hay until a threshing floor could be made. Helyar cleared and smoothed a circular area for this, building up the sides so that it could be flooded when the first frosts came. Bucket after bucket of water he and Vasilenna and the older boys poured on the flat area to freeze. This they did over and over again until the surface became a thick, flat sheet of ice. They placed the sheaves on the threshing floor and with homemade flails they beat the grain, winnowing it in the wind. Then Mother Zachary picked up the stalks to save for thatching.

The threshing over, Helyar set up a mill to grind the wheat into flour. Just a few weeks before the fire Vasilenna had made the first crusty, whole-wheat loaves of bread from their own milled flour.

The struggle and hardship the child could not know; but now as he lay on the neighbor's bed watching his mother, he heard her sigh deeply, and he noticed tears spilling over her cheeks.

"Why do you cry, Mamma?" the little fellow asked.

Vasilenna brushed the tears away. She smiled faintly at Jacob wrapped up on the bed. "I am thinking, my son. Do you remember the sweet nutty brown bread that came from our clay oven?" She paused. "But now the cabin—and everything—is gone." She wiped her eyes on the corner of the baby's blanket.

Father Zachary, coming in at that moment with the neighbor, placed another piece of the saved furniture in the already crowded cabin and came over to Mother Zachary.

"Don't cry, my Lenna," he said, patting her shoulder. "In the spring I will build you a new house. A better one this time, with a shingled roof."

"Yes, I know." Mother looked up at her husband. "How glad we should be that the fire didn't come in the night, especially in such cold weather. How glad we should be that we are all safe." Then she glanced at Jacob. "I hope the boy will not suffer from his ordeal."

Father Zachary adjusted his cap. "He is going to be all right. You will see. Have we not dedicated him to the priesthood?" He went out, leaving Mother with Mrs. Bilyuk, the children, and all the extra furniture piled in the neighbor's small cabin.

Jacob started to get off the bed.

"No, don't get off the bed," Mother cautioned.

And for the next several months Jacob and the Bilyuks' small children heard over and over again, "Don't get off the bed," or "No, you can't go outside. It is too cold. Play on the bed," or "Please stay in the corner or where you are. We are getting dinner ready. We can't have you underfoot."

Jacob became more and more fretful. His face and hands and feet burned and itched as the skin peeled off where he had been frostbitten. It seemed to the child that that winter would never end.

When at last the cold began to lessen, Father Zachary came with the news that he had borrowed a tent. He would fix a rough wood floor and siding in the tent, and the family could move in until the new house would be ready, he told Mother and Jacob.

"When will it be ready?" Jacob wanted to know.

"When the spring sunshine and warm winds dry the earth, we will

3

build," Father said. "In the meantime I will haul boards and shingles from the mill so everything will be in readiness."

Jacob watched Father unload the lumber in neat piles. Then at last one day neighbors from all around came to help in setting up the new home for the Zachary family.

In two weeks Jacob looked up at the beautiful two-story home—ready for the family to move into.

"Isn't it a fine house?" little Jacob shouted as he ran from one room to another, upstairs and down.

"A very fine house," Vasilenna Zachary agreed. "Large and light with all those windows. It is a blessing the old cabin burned down."

"Yes," Helyar nodded. "We have many blessings. There is the sawmill, and now a store has opened just two and a half miles from here where we can get our supplies without taking that long trip to Winnipeg. I will buy two steers to help haul supplies and logs. And, Lenna, the roads are so much better now. And the railroad goes beyond Winnipeg. Someday it will stretch from east to west in this great land. It passes within six miles of our place now. We are almost a part of Winnipeg." Helyar laughed as he spoke. "This year Charlie and I will find work in the mill. Alex and John can help with the garden, and soon even little Jacob will be old enough to help." Father placed his hand on Jacob's head.

"But I want to run and play." Jacob looked up at his father. "I want to watch the birds and the squirrels." Then he paused and wrinkled his brow. "Father," he went on, "why can't I climb in trees and leap from branch to branch like the squirrels do?"

"Ho!" Father Zachary's deep voice boomed. "What a question! A squirrel is a squirrel, and a boy is a boy."

Jacob went outside to puzzle over his father's words. "But why can't I be like a squirrel?" he asked himself. He ran out to the pasture and lay under a spreading tree. There were birds in the tree flitting from branch to branch. And he spied a squirrel too. Jacob watched the little fellow run out to the tip of a branch of the big tree; then, with a leap, the squirrel landed on the branch of a young, slender tree.

"I think I could do that," Jacob said aloud.

And one day he decided to try. He pulled himself up into a tree after a squirrel. The squirrel scampered up onto another branch. Jacob climbed after it. The squirrel raced far ahead of the boy, up into the slender branches. Jacob pulled himself up higher and higher. The branch began to bend and sway, but Jacob kept his eye on the squirrel. Suddenly he heard a rending, creaking sound. He felt himself falling. With a thud the ground seemed to come up to meet him. Everything went black.

Repeated flashes of light began to zig-zag before his eyes. Like summer lightning, he thought. He sat up and rubbed his fist across his eyes. What happened? he wondered, brushing away the leaves and the grass that clung to his shirt and hair. Had he died for a while? What about those lights flashing? And what about everything going black? Was that like being dead?

Several times after that when Jacob chased squirrels, he fell. Some times he blacked out and then had flashing lights dance before his eyes: It was a strange and puzzling experience.

"How do people die?" he asked his mother one day after having had a fall.

His mother dropped her hoe and stared at him. "Where did you ever get such a foolish question to ask? You are just a little boy. Stop thinking about how people die. Go and play, my son."

Jacob went away frowning. The question puzzled him for days. How do people die? At last he went to his mother again.

"Such things are not for a child to think about," she said, brushing him away. "Run along and play."

But the child's curiosity grew. The next day he came to his mother as she sat on the doorstep mending. "Mamma, where do people go after they die?"

Mother put down her mending. For a moment she sat with her hands in her lap. Then she looked at Jacob and said with a smile, "Why, people who are good go straight to heaven to live with God and the angels."

"What if they were bad?" Jacob went on.

"Then they go to hell," Mother Zachary answered.

"What is hell?" Jacob persisted.

Again Mother Zachary paused before answering. "Why, hell is a place where there is a huge fire. Devils keep it burning all the time. They put sulphur and pitch on the fire so it will never go out. It is a dreadful place."

"Why don't the bad people run away?"

"There is no place to run. It is too hot. The bad people burn there without end."

Jacob sat still, his chin resting in his cupped hands. "When do people go to hell or to heaven?" he asked.

"Just as soon as they die," Mother answered quickly.

"But—but how do they die? What is it like?" He sat up straight and looked up into his mother's face.

"Why, it's like going to sleep. Everything turns black—"

"Oh, I know. I died lots of times," Jacob spoke up. "But I didn't go anyplace. After it was all dark like you said, I saw flashes of light. Then—then, well, then, I woke up."

Mother Zachary grabbed Jacob's arms and turned him toward her. "How did all this happen?"

"Oh, in the woods. Come, I'll show you." Jacob jumped up and led her to the place under the tree where she could see the broken branches and even the impression his body had made in the grass where he had fallen.

Without a word she took Jacob by the hand and led him back to the house. Once inside, she set him on a chair facing her. "Jacob, you have been playing a very dangerous game." She shook her head as she spoke slowly. "I am surprised that you haven't broken an arm or a leg. You said you died. Well, you didn't, because you woke up again. If you had died you wouldn't have wakened; you would never have come home again. But, Son, if you keep on falling like that, someday you will die. Then you will never grow up to be a man." Mother paused.

Jacob saw tears in her eyes.

"Now promise me, Jacob, that you will never, never climb so you will fall like that again."

Jacob promised. But the question of death puzzled him more than ever. If the good ones went to heaven— Why did the bad ones have to stay in hell? And just what was it like?

6

That night he heard his parents talking about him and his questions about life and death. "If only we had a church here and a priest," he heard his mother say with a deep sigh.

"One of these days, Lenna," Father Zachary said. "One of these days we will have a fine Greek Catholic church right in our own community." But then they turned out the lamp and Jacob heard no more.

Jacob had never gone to church so far as he could remember. In a special place in the parlor his parents had an image of Mary and the Christ Child. And among the pictures that hung on the wall was one of the "Holy Mother" and one of the blessed Saviour, a young man with sad eyes, exposing his heart encircled with thorns. Jacob had been taught that this blessed Saviour had suffered for His people, but he was not sure how or why.

It was not until he had his eighth birthday that a church was completed in the community. Jacob went with his father to the first service. Standing in the doorway, he looked down the aisle to the shrines and lighted candles. There stood the priest in his splendid robes. Father Zachary started down the aisle toward the priest, and Jacob followed, hardly daring to breathe. Father knelt down before the altar, and Jacob knelt too.

The priest put a covering over Jacob's head. "Now you must tell me all your sins," the priest said, placing his hands on the boy's shoulders.

"What are sins?" Jacob asked.

"Wrong things we do. Have you told any lies?"

Jacob paused to think. "I—I don't think so."

"Have you stolen anything?" the priest went on.

"No, I do not steal," Jacob answered firmly.

"Have you stolen cookies from your mother?"

"No. I don't steal," he replied again. "Nobody steals at our house."

The priest lifted the covering from Jacob's head. "You may go, my son."

Jacob got up feeling strangely dissatisfied. But the rituals and the feasting that followed made him forget. The services brought all the people in the community together so that they could show off their clothes and their possessions, and they could exchange gossip and news, and eat.

Jacob stuffed himself on the special feast days. The women brought *pyrohy*, a dumpling stuffed with potato and cottage cheese or meat, and served with onions and sour cream. Then there was always *borsch*, a soup made from grated beets, potatoes, onions, carrots, and other vegetables. And no Greek Catholic feast could ever be complete without the special bread, a kind of coffee cake, the braided sweet dough full of dried fruits and covered with poppy seeds. Jacob rolled his tongue over his lips as he thought of the food, especially that made by his mother. And her wild strawberry and wild raspberry wines were the talk of the whole community! Yes, it was good to have a new church around which to center the social and religious life. But Jacob wished he could understand more of the things the priest taught.

Someday, he decided, he would have a talk with the priest and find the answers to the things that puzzled him. But Mother Zachary kept telling him he was too young to think so many serious thoughts.

"Come eat the good food and enjoy the good company. When you are older, you can understand better," she said.

One day Father Zachary came home with the news that a school would soon open in Foley, two and a half miles away. Alex and Jacob could go to school; but since John and Charlie, the two older boys, were already working in the sawmill, they would not need to go.

On the first day of school Jacob got up before dawn. He wanted to be the first to arrive. Perhaps at school he would get the answers to many of the questions that bothered him. And he would learn English! Then he would be able to talk to the lady at the mill who always gave him bread and molasses when he went there. She chattered away to him in English, smiling all the while, but Jacob could not understand a word she said. He dressed and was waiting when Alex came into the kitchen.

"Boys!" Father Zachary's voice stopped Alex and Jacob when they were about to leave the house. "School is a place for children to be good and listen to the teacher. So do whatever she tells you. When you get to school, sit where the teacher tells you and listen to her. Pay no attention to anyone else." Then looking straight at Jacob he added,

"You are not going to chase squirrels, but to learn English. Remember that. And, Jacob, your name in English will be Jack."

The boys nodded, and Jacob gulped. School might not be so much fun after all. He frowned at the thought.

But when he arrived at the one-room schoolhouse and saw the teacher, Eva Brown, he felt all soft inside. She was the prettiest person he had ever seen. He vowed he would do anything for her. She spoke to the children, and her voice sounded sweet and bubbly like Mother's raspberry wine.

"Good morning, boys and girls," Miss Brown said, looking straight at Jacob.

And Jacob, not understanding a word of English, but knowing he must say something, jumped to his feet and blurted out, "Jack Zachary."

The children laughed, but the teacher put her hand on his shoulder and smiled down at him. And Jack Zachary knew for sure that school would be the best place on earth, next to home and Mother, with Miss Brown as his teacher.

From that day, Jacob's name became Jack to his teachers, school mates, brothers, and sister Mary. Only his parents called him Jacob.

At the end of the first school year Miss Brown left. No one ever took her place in Jack's heart. The following year he began to lose interest in school right from the start. The children became unruly; the teacher had no discipline. When the older ones were saucy or rebellious, she sat down and cried. Before the end of that school year she returned to Winnipeg, and a new teacher came to the Foley school, a quick-tempered Scot, the children soon found out, with a dark complexion and a black, stiffly waxed handlebar moustache.

He smiled little and said even less. That first morning Jack sat back in his seat to watch and see what would happen when the children whispered and coughed and threw spitwads. The teacher said nothing about it all morning. At noon he went to the mill for lunch. When he returned, Jack noticed a bundle of laths under his arm.

The teacher called the children into the schoolroom. He made a speech about school being a place for learning, and he intended it to be so. There was to be no nonsense. Jack decided the teacher meant what he said. He also learned, by observing those who did not pay attention to the teacher, what the laths were for. By evening the bundle had been pretty well broken up. The next morning the teacher brought another bundle of laths. In a few days the school became a model of deportment. That year jack began his formal learning. He began to read and write English.

The fourth teacher at the Foley school was Ukrainian. Most of his teaching he did in Ukrainian, and Jack wanted more than anything else to learn English. He rebelled.

"If that teacher stays," he told his mother, "I am not going to stay in school. I'll run away."

"Now, Jacob," Mother Zachary remonstrated, "you are joking. You must listen to the teacher."

But one cold morning in December as he and Alex and Mary prepared for school, Jack hid his books upstairs and came down with his empty schoolbag over his shoulder. While Mother Zachary finished preparing breakfast, Jack sneaked a few slices of bread and some meat into his bag along with his school lunch.

"You and Mary go on ahead," he suggested to Alex when they were ready to leave.

Waiting until Alex and Mary would have reached the crossroad, Jack started out. He took the road that led to the main highway rather than the one that led to the school. Two miles down the road he came to Dragon's Store. The proprietor, standing in the doorway, greeted him.

"Jack, how come you're not in school?" "Well, I need some rubbers," the boy answered. "My feet get cold walking in these moccasins."

He went into the store, and the man fitted him with rubbers and charged them to the family account. Jack said goodbye and went on his way, taking the main road to Winnipeg.

He drew his cap down as far as he could over his ears. The wind pierced through his thick mackinaw. He swung his arms back and forth and clapped his mittened hands to keep warm as he hurried on. From time to time he cupped his hands over his mouth and nose and blew a puff of steamy breath to warm his face.

By lunchtime he found his food frozen solid. He tried to eat as he walked on, blowing on the bread to soften it a little. In the late afternoon he reached Pleasant Home. Forty miles yet to go to Winnipeg! His feet felt numb, his legs weary; but he plodded on. Just as the sun was setting he came to a settlement along the highway. The sun's rays gleamed on the windows of the homes; plumes of smoke rose from the chimneys, and Jack began to think of home—of Mother setting the table for supper, and of the warm, cheery kitchen. He was cold and hungry. Should he turn back? He gnawed a little more of his frozen bread.

No, he would make his way in the world. He would go on. Through the deepening cold and twilight Jack trudged on past the last house and through a wooded area. Then he heard the weird howl of timber wolves.

He listened and shivered. But he heard another sound. Sleighbells! Turning to look back, he saw a team approaching. Coming abreast of him, the team stopped; a big man, bundled against the weather, his face almost covered by a thick scarf, called out: "Where are you going, boy?"

"I'm looking for work," Jack answered.

"I need a boy to do my chores," the man said. "Get in the sleigh and come home with me. My name's Campbell."

Jack, cold, weary, and hungry, got into the sleigh. He puzzled over the word "chores." Whatever did that mean? The word sounded a little like "church." Perhaps the man wanted him to perform some religious duties for him, but at that moment he was too weary to care.

Mr. Campbell soon turned in at a farm. "Here we are," he announced in a loud voice. "Come on in."

Jack followed the man into the house.

"I picked this kid up on the road," he announced to the family. "He's going to help with the chores." He introduced the four older girls and then the younger children.

Jack looked around the room. There were electric lights in the house. He had never before seen a house wired for electricity. All the room in the house seemed to have the same kind of lights!

After supper he followed Mr. Campbell out to the barn where he

11

learned that "chores" on the Campbell farm were no more religious than anywhere else. But here he had a warm place to stay and good food. He decided to stay and work for Mr. Campbell and earn some money.

He sent word home to his parents telling them of his whereabouts and telling his mother not to worry. But after a few weeks on the farm he began to get homesick. He wanted to be home for the Greek Catholic Christmas holiday season. A few days before January 7, when the festivities would begin, Jack took leave of the Campbells. With seven dollars in wages in his pocket and more English in his head than he had before, Jack started home.

He walked the same way as he had come, stopping at the store to buy a piece of dress material for his mother in a pretty blue pattern. The nearer he came to home, the faster he walked. It seemed he had been away so long.

The sun had set when he turned in the gate, and strode up to the kitchen door.

"Jack's home!" His sister Mary jumped up from where she had been sitting when she heard the door open and saw him standing in the doorway.

Everyone turned and stared at him. Then Mother Zachary hurried over and threw her arms around him.

"Here is a present for you, Mother." Jack handed her the package shyly.

"Thank you, Son. Thank you." Her voice sounded a little shaky. As she opened the package everyone started talking at once.

At last Alex came over and stood by Jack, clapping him on the back. "We've got a good teacher now. A Miss Burroughs. How about staying home and going back to school?"

And before school started after the holiday season, Jack decided to return to school. With Miss Burroughs's help, his lessons came easy. But by the end of the school year he had his twelfth birthday, and he was expected now to help support the family.

That summer the crops suffered from drought. Each passing day the gardens and wheat fields withered a little more under the blazing sun. Forest fires broke out all around the small community where the

Zacharys lived. The brassy sun shone through the smoky, acrid air, and soot and cinders floated down on fields and freshly washed clothes as they hung limp on clotheslines. Wherever neighbors met, they talked of the drought and of the total harvest loss they feared.

On a Sunday in mid-July the priest announced that he would conduct a special mass that evening at seven and he would pray for rain. "The mass will cost the church twenty-five dollars," he announced to the waiting congregation. "Perhaps we shall have rain!"

That evening Jack trudged along the dusty road to the church with his father. He thought about the drought and about prayer and about God. Would God answer the priest's prayer and send rain?

Inside the dimly lit church, the smell of burning wax and incense almost overcame the boy. Then the priest appeared.

In a solemn voice he announced, "This is a special mass. We will pray for rain, and maybe we will have rain and maybe not. That is in the hands of God. We cannot be sure."

Jack carried out the motions expected of him in the service. But many questions filled his mind. The rain is in the hands of God. But the money is in the hands of the church. And what do the people get? He tried to put the thoughts out of his head. It was wrong to think such thoughts. He tried to listen as the service went on and on.

At last the people filed out of the church, and Jack walked home with his father and a neighbor in the gathering twilight.

"Father," the boy blurted out as they walked along, "Father Androchovich seemed so positive about the cost of the mass, and yet so doubtful about the rain. This does not seem right. I think if—"

"Hush!" his father hissed, clapping his hand over Jack's mouth.

But the boy wriggled free. "But—but—I don't see why we have to pay if we don't get rain," he persisted.

"It is a sin to question the father's intention," the neighbor spoke up. "You must not ever question that, Jack Zachary."

"You know, Jacob," his father reminded him, "you must always remember that your mother and I have dedicated you to a holy mission. You must always remember that the priest stands in the place of God to us."

Jack dared not speak of the matter again, but he couldn't help wondering about a God who drove such doubtful bargains. Or was it the priest who was so uncertain? But wasn't the priest supposed to know God?

While the whole community scanned the heavens for rain, Jack Zachary watched with particular interest. When the rain did come, it was too little and too late to save the crops. Jack said nothing, but he felt they had been cheated. Just who to blame he wasn't sure. But as time passed, the confused doubts were gradually pushed to the back of his mind.

2

Across the River

The summer Jack became thirteen and Alex sixteen, Father Zachary called the two boys to him. "My sons, here is ten dollars. It is time for you to learn more self-reliance and to take more responsibility. You will go to Winnipeg and find work. Come home in the fall and be sure to bring at least ten dollars back with you."

Mother, with a tear on her cheek, bade the boys good-bye as they started for the railway station six miles away. Jack swallowed a large lump in his throat as he turned to wave to his mother standing in the doorway of their home. Then without looking back again he trudged along beside Alex to the station, where they bought their tickets for the city. Alex showed Jack the money left. Less than eight dollars!

Arriving in the city, the boys found their way to the employment office and asked for work.

"You are too young. We can't use boys," the man told them. And day after day they heard the same words over and over. At night they slept in boxcars, and in the daytime they bought as little food as they could possibly get along on.

One day Alex pulled the few coins left out of his pocket. "I don't know what we are going to do," he said, turning his pockets inside out. "How long can we make thirty cents last?"

That night they went to sleep in the boxcar hungry. Sometime in the night Jack awakened to the steady clackety-clack sound of moving train wheels. He shook Alex.

"Wake up! We're moving!"

Jack peered through the cracks in the car trying to see if he could

15

recognize any landmarks, but he could see little in the darkness. Finally the train stopped, and the boys scrambled out of the car.

By now the darkness had started to fade. Looking around, Jack could see that they were out in the country, but at that early hour there were no signs of life.

"We might as well start walking." Jack shrugged his shoulders. And the two boys started down the road. After a time they came to a small station. Saint Norbert, the sign read.

"That's the name of the French settlement beyond Winnipeg," Alex said. "What are we going to do? Nobody will hire us to work, and I'm starving."

Jack saw a tear trickle down his brother's cheek.

"Maybe we'd better go home." Alex's voice broke.

But Jack shook his head. "We'd have to walk, and we're too hungry. Besides, we don't have ten dollars to give back to Father. Come on, let's keep going." Then after a pause, he added, "Maybe we should pray to Saint Nicholas. He might help us."

Together the boys repeated the prayer their mother had taught them when they were children, "Merciful holy father, Saint Nicholas, we appeal to your heart full of mercy. Have pity upon us. Oh, holy saint, help us in our time of need."

A mile or so down the road the boys came upon a gang of men working on the railroad tracks. "Look!" Jack pointed. "There's a pile of shovels over there. Let's watch our chance and start working with the men. After we've worked they'll surely pay us."

Jack and Alex, unnoticed by the men, picked out two shovels and started to work. Halfway through the morning the timekeeper came along.

"What's your number?" he asked Jack.

"Don't have a number," the boy mumbled, hardly looking up. "Well, you're 390," the timekeeper said, writing something on his pad. "And you're 391," he told Alex.

Alex and Jack looked at each other and grinned as the man walked away.

At noon the men knocked off for lunch, and the boys walked to a store close by and bought a stale loaf of rye bread for four cents. Jack tried to break off a piece of the loaf. At last he knocked it on a stone and the loaf broke in two. At the pump of a watering trough the boys soaked the bread so that they could eat it.

Looking at the small piece still in his hand, Jack decided to save that piece of bread for the next meal. The twenty-six cents left of their ten dollars might have to stretch a long way, he thought as he put the small hard piece of bread in his pocket.

All afternoon the boys worked with the men on the railroad tracks. At the close of the day they found another boxcar, and after the hard day's work they fell asleep exhausted. Morning came all too soon. Sleepily they started down the road to work.

Why did men passing them seem to stare and laugh? Jack wondered.

Then one passerby called, "Where did you sleep last night?"

Mystified, Jack looked at Alex and Alex looked at Jack. Then they burst out laughing.

"If you could only see yourself," Alex doubled over.

"That goes double," Jack said, a little disgusted. "Your face is as black as soot, except for the whites of your eyes and your teeth. You sure look funny!"

"We slept in a coal car last night, I guess. We'd better clean up a little," Alex suggested.

They wiped themselves off as best they could on the dew-wet grass in the empty lot; then they went on their way. No one in the road gang seemed to worry about a little coal dust.

"Guess we've got ourselves a steady job," Alex told Jack on the third day with the railroad crew.

But that afternoon the supervisor came over to the boys. "What are you doing working here?" he roared at Jack.

"I work as hard as anyone here," Jack answered quickly.

"You rascal! Do you want me to lose my job? It's against the law to hire kids." He scribbled something on a piece of paper.

"Aw, leave the kid alone," one of the men spoke up. "He works harder than the rest of us. He never takes a break."

"I'm sorry," the supervisor said. "It's against the law."

"If he goes, I go too," Alex spoke up, and put down his shovel.

The supervisor scribbled again and handed the paper to the boys. "Sorry! Take your time cards to the timekeeper."

The timekeeper wrote out a slip stating that they had worked so many hours for three days at seventeen cents an hour. "Take this to the pay clerk," the timekeeper told the boys.

The pay clerk took the slips. "OK. You'll get your money in three days. Come back then. You'll get $5.90 each."

"Oh, please, sir," Jack pleaded, "we have only eighteen cents and we are hungry. We can't wait three days."

Finally the pay clerk led them to another office where they received their pay.

Jack looked at the money in his hand. "Well, maybe we'd better go home now. We've got more than ten dollars together."

Alex frowned. "By the time we buy our tickets for home we won't have ten dollars left. Let's go back to the employment office in town once more."

So the boys made their way back to the city. At the employment office Jack noticed an ad on the bulletin board. "Alex, read this. They need workers to clear land at Kirkland Park, it says. 'Applicants must report in person and bring their own axes.'" Jack read on.

Without comment the boys hurried down the street to the nearest hardware store, where they each purchased an ax. Then they went out to the Kirkland Park area.

"You're too young. We can't use boys. You'd be cutting yourselves with those new axes," the supervisor told them. Jack felt indignant. He knew he was a better woodsman than most. But it was useless to argue. He put his ax over his shoulder and, followed by Alex, trudged on down the road.

"Maybe we should go home, Alex," Jack spoke slowly. "Father won't put us out just because we haven't ten dollars."

"OK. If we don't find work by tomorrow—" Alex began as Jack nudged him.

"There's a man walking right behind us. We better let him pass," Jack said in an undertone.

The man, coming abreast of the boys, smiled. "Hello! You boys looking for work?"

They stared at the brown-skinned man with the straight black hair. He had come upon them so silently in his moccasined feet that he had almost startled them.

"An Indian!" Jack whispered to Alex.

"Sh-sh!" Alex warned. Then he turned to the man. "We sure are looking for work."

"I have a contract to clear land," the Indian said. "I pay $1.50 a day, and board."

"We'll try it," Jack agreed, having hastily looked to Alex for agreement.

"My name is Isadore," the man said. "Follow me."

Jack and Alex followed the man along the road for some distance; then they turned to follow a path through the woods. Jack remembered stories he had heard of Indians scalping people. The boys held a whispered conversation. They decided to unwrap their axes and hold them ready. They were ever on the alert for unexpected movements from behind trees, and they walked cautiously to defend themselves in case of ambush.

Much to Jack's relief they soon came upon a clearing where two tents were pitched. A man leaned over a frypan beside an open fire. He grunted a welcome and went on with the meal preparation while Isadore and the two boys looked on. Then the man cooking dished up the food onto tin plates—fried potatoes, salt meat, and hot biscuits.

At sight and smell of the food, Jack lost his fear, and Alex followed suit as they fell to work on the first hot meal they'd had in several days. A bowl of Mother's homemade *borsch* or a plate of *pyrohy* would probably have tasted no better than the meal the boys ate that evening.

Supper over, the Indian asked Jack to accompany him to get some supplies from a French farmer who lived nearby. There he bought a bag of potatoes and refilled a jug that he had brought with him. Jack wondered about the contents of the jug from which Isadore took frequent swigs, until the Indian's steps became more and more unsteady. When they came to a small stream, spanned by a foot-wide plank, Jack walked across and started up the opposite bank when he heard a splash behind him. Turning to look, he saw Isadore floundering in the water. Jack set down the potatoes and fished Isadore from the

19

water. The rest of the way home Jack not only carried the potatoes and the jug, but steadied Isadore as well.

Next morning they began to clear land. Day after day they worked hard from morning till night, but the work was not unpleasant, and it did prove to be profitable. By the end of the summer Jack and Alex had over $100 each.

When they returned home to Rockwood, Jack noted with pleasure the happiness on Mother's face on their safe arrival, and Father's satisfaction when he learned how well his sons had done.

The boys stayed home that fall to help clear more farmland. The Zacharys' once-wooded homestead now became a farm of hayfields and cultivated lands. It was during the Christmas vacation that year that some cousins from Sandy Lake, a Ukrainian settlement to the east, came to visit the Zacharys and persuaded Helyar to sell the farm and move to Sandy Lake. The soil, they said, was rich and fertile with hardly a rock on it, quite in contrast to Rockwood, which lived up to its name. The following March, the Zachary family bought a farm from a German settler and, having sold their original homestead, moved to the new farm with a good farmhouse.

After clearing more land on the new farm, Jack and Alex once more set out to find work. This time the railroad hired them properly, Alex on the gang laying new tracks, and Jack as a cookee, peeling potatoes, washing dishes, and setting tables. Jack's wages were seventeen cents an hour. The boss noticed his faithfulness in all his tasks, and when there was an opening, Jack got the job of cook's assistant. And a little later as foreman of the trimming gang, with thirty-two men under him, Jack Zachary became the youngest foreman on the Canadian Pacific Railroad.

Since the work on the railroad was seasonal, Jack and Alex returned to the farm in the winter. Jack, now almost twenty, with deep-set, searching blue eyes, medium-tall in height and of a husky build, had the rugged look of a farm boy, the bronzed skin, the unruly brown hair, the square hands well acquainted with hoe and ax. But the time was near for Jack to leave home to enter the seminary and prepare for the priesthood. From early childhood he had been brought up to believe in his special mission. And always there seemed to be with him a nameless longing to know God.

The Zacharys had a Bible in the house. But Jack had never read it. The priest had so many times said the Book could not be understood by the laity. So the Book lay on the shelf, a kind of holy relic. Jack had read any other worthwhile literature that he came upon, especially anything religious. One day he happened to see a friend with a book by the evangelist Billy Sunday.

"A heretic's book!" Jack exclaimed, thumbing through the pages. But it intrigued him; so he borrowed it and read it and found himself strangely warmed by the zeal of the heretic preacher who had vowed that he would "preach Christ until hell freezes over."

Often after reading the book he found himself thinking about several things that had bothered him in years past. He spoke to no one about them. Someday—someday soon he would find the answers to his many questions. Surely at the seminary the questions would be answered.

That year Charles married a girl from the settlement. Charles and Pearl, his wife, stayed on the Zachary home place. But since John would marry soon, Father Zachary called the family together for a council.

"Boys," he said, "we will have to get more land. There is not enough room here on the old place for three families. We must buy another farm."

"But where in Sandy Lake?" John asked. "There's no farm for sale anywhere around here."

"That's true, but we must have more space." Helyar drummed his fingertips on the table. Then he looked up, shoved his chair back, and said, "I think we will have to cross the river."

For a moment not a sound was heard in the room.

Then Jack drew a cigarette from his pocket and lit it. He breathed in the smoke, then slowly blew it out. With narrowed eyes he looked at his father. "You know that is not Catholic country across the river."

"Yes, yes," Father replied. "I know very well. But buying land from people doesn't mean getting religion from them. A man can live among neighbors and mind his own business."

Again there was silence in the room. Then Helyar Zachary spoke up again. "Jack, you will be the one to go across the river. You will look for a farm with at least 320 acres, land enough for you and John and his wife and Alex. It would be good, too, to have a house and a barn already on the land."

Jack set out on his bicycle one warm October morning. As he pedaled, he thought of the people across the river. He had met heretics before. He had talked to them. Some were even nice people. But to live across the river among these people not of the Catholic faith would be something else.

Once he was across the river, it took only a short while to find just the place he wanted. A farm owned by a Mr. Croft had the right acreage; the land was well fenced; it had a barn, a well, a large house, and even a telephone. A good road passed the farm and went on to the little town of Moline, two miles away. Best of all, Mr. Croft wanted to sell the place and at a reasonable figure. Jack hurried back home to Sandy Lake to tell the family of his find.

Almost before Jack had finished telling about the Croft farm, the decision had been to buy the place. Jack phoned Mr. Croft at once to tell him the deal was on. The Zacharys, John and his wife-to-be, Annie, with Alex and Jack would cross the river into heretic country.

3

The Auction

Early in the spring the boys began to take stock of what they would take with them from the home place at Sandy Lake to the farm across the river. Father could let them have four horses, but they would need a gang plow and a seed drill. They watched the ads in the newspapers and finally found a notice about a sale on a farm some seventeen miles away. And it was decided that Jack and John should go to the sale.

"Keep on your guard, boys," Father warned as Jack and John hitched the horse to the cutter. "I've heard the man who is selling is a Protestant."

Mother Zachary, coming out of the house with a foot warmer, exclaimed, "A Protestant!" She set the brick charcoal burner down in the sleigh quickly and crossed herself.

The boys got into the cutter and pulled the buffalo robe up over their knees.

"Don't worry," Jack called, snapping the reins lightly on the horse's back. The sleigh bells jingled as they drove off over the crusted snow.

They arrived at the farm at eleven, just as the sale was about to start. Some of the larger farm machinery could be seen in front of the barn and some by the house. Smith Russell, the auctioneer, bustled about amid the display of furniture and other household goods set out on the broad veranda across the front of the house. Jack watched the auctioneer out of the corner of his eye. He'd heard the man was an Irish Protestant who liked nothing better than to needle Catholics.

The man went over to a bookcase and drew from it a large black, goldlettered book. Holding it up he shouted, "Now all ye foine

Catholics, we'll begin the sale with the best article Mr. Jameson possessed, and that is the Bible."

A chorus of "boos" arose from the crowd.

The auctioneer turned the book this way and that. "It's got a ginuine leather bindin' stamped with the solid gold. Who'll start me with tin dollars?"

A slight murmur went through the onlookers.

"How much am I offered? Start me anywheres." The auctioneer looked around, all the while talking steadily. "If this book don't go, the sale don't go. What am I offered? Start me anywheres."

Jack began to worry about the sale. Suppose the auctioneer meant what he said. What if the sale didn't go on? Seventeen miles was a long way to come for nothing. "Twenty-five cents," Jack blurted out.

"Sold!" And before Jack could say another word, the auctioneer tossed the book into his hands. In something of a daze he paid the clerk his quarter, and stole off through the crowd to where they'd left the horse and cutter. He'd have a quick look at the book and then return to the sale, he decided.

But before he reached the cutter he met the elder of the Sandy Lake church. The older man took off his mitts and felt of the book in Jack's hand. "You still got a bargain," he said. "This is real leather and will make good patches for gloves and mitts."

Jack hurried on. He didn't want the man to take the book and look inside and perhaps condemn it before he had even had a chance to look at it.

When he arrived at the cutter, Jack got in and settled his feet on the warm heater under the buffalo robe. Then he took a good look at his new acquisition. It was not a Bible after all, he noted, but a book called *Bible Readings for the Home Circle*. Well, he had no home circle, not being married, but he still wanted to read the book. Of course, he would have to be careful with a Protestant book. He decided to open the book near the beginning, and take a quick glance. If what he saw was too shocking, he would shut the book at once and never open it again.

Jack stuck both index fingers into the book. He paused. One of these days he would be going away to study for the priesthood. A future priest should never take a chance on heresy, he mused, not even to peek, but— "If I open it close to the beginning," he reasoned again, "I'll take less chance. I won't go in deep. Just one little glance."

He opened the book.

A familiar, reassuring picture of Christ on the cross with the thieves on either side met his glance. The title of the chapter struck him as strange indeed. He read it aloud. "'Salvation Only Through Christ.'" Over and over Jack repeated the words. "Is it possible? Is there a clearer way to salvation? A way through Christ? Does this mean—?" So absorbed he became that he didn't realize he was talking out loud.

He noted that the book was something like a catechism, being made up of questions and answers. But every answer was a Bible text.

"Is there salvation through any other name?" he read. Acts 4:12 was the answer. "Neither is there salvation in any other: for there is none other name under heaven given among men, whereby we must be saved."

He read on. "For what purpose did Christ come into the world?" 1 Timothy 1:15. "This is a faithful saying, and worthy of all acceptation, that Christ Jesus came into the world to save sinners.'" On and on he read in the book.

A hand on his shoulder roused him. "Well, come on. Let's be going." John stood beside the cutter.

"Huh?" Jack looked up startled. "What's that? Have they come to the plow and the seed drill yet?"

"Plow and seed drill, you donkey. The sale is over. You've been riveted to that book for four hours."

Jack took a deep breath and looked around. "Well, let's get going then." He moved over to make room for John in the cutter.

All the way home Jack sat in deep thought. He hardly noticed when John spoke to him.

"It was such a good plow and went so cheap, also the drill. And you were nowhere to be seen," John repeated.

"Must have been something wrong with them," Jack spoke slowly.

"They were in good condition," retorted John.

But Jack had gone back to his deep thinking: "Where am I going?

27

Salvation is only through Christ. There is no other name. Have I been attached to other names? Oh, please, God, help me!"

"We've wasted the trip—all for nothing." John's voice came as from a great distance. "I'll never take you to a sale again. The idea of buying a Bible and reading it all afternoon! Why, Sunday is the time for that."

But John's reproaches scarcely touched him. Jack was like a man who, lost and hungry in a dark forest, sees ahead an opening in the trees and a path of golden sunlight shining through.

4

Rain Without Clouds

The first part of April, 1917, the Zachary boys moved to the new farm and soon began seeding the land. Some three weeks after the move, Jack and Alex with a horse and buggy went to Rivers, a railway center, to get some supplies. As they tied the horse to the hitching post in front of the general store, a middle-aged man with a kindly face stopped to talk to them. They soon found out that he was one of the Protestants whom they had been taught to avoid. His name was Brown. He asked where they lived. Yes, he knew the place, he told the boys. He even knew the homesteaders who had cleared it thirty years before. He asked about the acreage, the number of horses they had, the size of their family.

"Three brothers?" he said. "I'll tell you, boys. Why don't one of you come with me and help me with my spring planting? Then later I'll let you use as many horses as you need to break new land and plow summer fallow at your place."

The boys went back of the wagon and discussed the proposition in Ukrainian. The man seemed friendly and a quite harmless heretic, they agreed. Three or four weeks wouldn't do any harm, neither would a little extra money. It was decided that Jack, being the youngest, was the one to go.

That afternoon Mr. Brown and Jack drove along in the pleasant spring sunshine, talking of farming and crops and horses.

"Mr. Brown's a very pleasant man. Nothing to fear from him," Jack mused, as he thought about being so close to a Protestant.

Two miles south of Harding, Manitoba, Mr. Brown stopped at a well-kept farmhouse. "Here we are, Jack," he said, "and it's just about suppertime. Come in and meet the family."

Jack liked Mrs. Brown immediately. She had a smile that made him feel right at home. "I'm sure you must be hungry," she said. "We're just ready to sit down. Annie, bring another plate," she said to the hired girl. Then she introduced Jack to the four children.

When the group sat down at the large table, all bowed their heads as Mr. Brown asked the blessing. And Jack made the sign of the cross three times as he'd been taught. As he ate, he remembered that he had to cross himself at the close of the meal also. Maybe he'd better not. These heretics would probably laugh at him, he reasoned. But Father Keluznyatsky had said that he must never be ashamed of his religion, especially in front of heretics. No, he must be faithful. Having finished eating, he glanced furtively about, then quickly made the required sign. To Jack's surprise the whole family hushed their conversation respectfully, and there was not a smile or a giggle from even the youngest child.

Through succeeding days the new farmhand watched the Brown family with interest. All his life he had been taught that only Catholics would enter into the kingdom of heaven. Surely Peter would never open the gate to heretics. But the more he watched the Browns, the more he admired their Christian lives. There was such a spirit of cooperation among them. They were Methodists, he learned. They not only read the Bible; its principles were illustrated in their daily lives. How could God cast such people into eternal fire? Jack admitted that they were more like saints than heretics; much better, in fact, than his own family or the neighbors he had known.

One rainy day when the men had come in a little early for dinner, Mr. Brown sat in his rocker to read while Annie Turner, the hired girl, set the table in the large kitchen. Annie reached into the oven to get the plates that had been placed there to warm. Jack saw her hurry to the table with the hot dishes, but she tripped just behind the rocking chair, and the dishes fell with a crash.

"Good night!" screamed Annie, and tears filled her eyes.

Slowly Mr. Brown turned his head. "Why, good morning, Annie," he said smiling.

Mrs. Brown came running from the pantry clucking soothingly as she helped pick up the pieces. "It's quite all right," she said quietly. "Why, Annie, the sole of your shoe is loose. And see here, the tack has come out of the linoleum. John, you must fix this. I'll be falling here myself next."

In the corner Jack had been watching everything. How foolish scolding would have been. It wouldn't have mended a single plate. But here indeed was the patience of the saints. "They have some power that keeps them on an even keel," he mused. "I wish I had it. I don't care what they call it, but it must come from God."

Each morning Jack got up early to build a fire in the kitchen cookstove. On the table or on a chair Mrs. Brown's Bible lay open. He knew she often stopped in her work during the day to read a verse or two. Now as Jack went about his early morning work he stole glances at that open Book. Some of the verses, he noted, were marked in red. And much to his surprise he found the verses were the same ones he had read in his book, *Bible Readings*.

Each day Jack became more and more disturbed. How could God burn good heretics? Finally he could find but one solution. He must convert these people to the Catholic faith. After all, would not he himself also be in danger of hellfire if he did not try to save these souls?

But how should he start? He trembled whenever he thought of it. He needed courage and wisdom, but he could only approach God through the set forms he had learned from his prayer book, and there were no prayers to fit his case. Only too well he remembered the warning never to add to or subtract from these prayers. Nevertheless, despite his fears, Jack's determination to win the Browns became stronger. He pictured himself throughout eternity gazing in horror over the battlements of heaven into the awful abyss of hell, into the tortured faces of his friends. Oh, he must save them! He would speak to Mr. Brown at the first opportunity.

From that time on Jack watched for a moment to be alone with the man. He imagined that it would be simple enough to point out the heresy, and since Mr. Brown was so honest and good, he would immediately see the light and then enlighten his family. One Saturday in early June as they finished dinner, Mr. Brown said, "Jack will you hitch Molly and Joe to the wagon? I'll go down with you to bring some oats from the lower section."

At last! His heart pounded. Here was the chance he had been waiting for! He hurried out to hitch up the horses.

In record time Jack drove the "three-decked" wagon, used for hauling oats, up to the kitchen door. Mr. Brown climbed up into the seat, and Jack handed him the reins. With a cluck from the driver, the team started. Then, fearful of losing his nerve if he waited another minute, Jack plunged in. "Oh, sir, I feel so sorry for you. You will never get through the gates of heaven if—" Jack stopped, feeling quite miserable now saying such things to his employer.

Mr. Brown turned his kind eyes on the boy. "Jack," he said, "you are trying so hard to live a Christian life. It is our duty to help you."

Jack's mouth felt suddenly dry. His heart pounded. It would be dreadful if he should become a heretic. "Oh, no! Please, God, not that," Jack thought.

Mr. Brown went on. "Jack, do you really believe that Christian living consists in carrying a cross around your neck as you do? If I thought that was all that is required, I would make a cross weighing ten pounds and tie it around my neck with logging chains. The cross you carry is so small that I'm sure you don't feel it."

Jack's face reddened. He had never thought these heretics noticed his cross.

"Jack, how can you know that the sins you confess to the priest are really forgiven?" Mr. Brown went on. "You'd better make sure. No sinner will enter heaven. Our sins must be forgiven while we are here on earth. Christ alone can cleanse us from our sins, the Bible says. Sins are the transgression of God's word, not man's word, in the judgment each man must answer for himself. No earthly priest can substitute. The priests, cardinals, even the pope himself, must depend on Christ alone for salvation."

Though many of these words sounded familiar, for he had read them in his "auction" book, Jack had never applied them so clearly as this. The mention of the pope as needing a Saviour horrified him. "Surely not the pope!" Jack reasoned silently. "He is holy. He is like

Christ on earth." Jack decided he must not listen to these terrible things. Surely God would strike him dead.

They reached the lower section, and Mr. Brown fell silent as they began to work in the pleasant summer sunshine. But in Jack's mind a terrible storm raged. All afternoon he loaded the oats, working automatically, while his mind struggled with the giant ideas that had attacked him.

As the two men drove home in the late afternoon, Jack found himself face to face with one big question. Though he might rebel against this Christ who must stand supreme, he could not avoid the looming question blocking his every escape route like a granite mountain: "Jack, are your sins forgiven?" Despite countless confessionals, he didn't know. Why, if his sins were not forgiven, he was still a sinner, and not even Saint Peter would have the authority to admit a Catholic sinner into heaven any more than a Protestant heretic. A sinner would make trouble in heaven. That was why God cast out the devil in the first place, he'd read in his book. He must do something. He must know of a surety that his sins were forgiven.

That night as he sat down to supper, he felt haunted and defeated. He ate little. He looked at the happy faces around the table and wondered, "Do they know their sins are forgiven? Even if they don't confess to a priest?" He wished he dared ask them.

After finishing the evening chores, Jack went to his room with his prayer books. Carefully he scrutinized each prayer, but there were none that filled his present need. Over and over he kept repeating the prayers he had always known, and finally, quite exhausted, he lay down, but not to rest. All night his thoughts scrambled like a squirrel in a cage.

Very early as Sunday morning began to dawn, Jack got up quietly and slipped out of the house while the family slept. He fed and watered the thirty work horses; then he returned to his room to get his best prayer book, *The Path to Heaven*. He slipped it into his pocket, put on his cap, and stole silently out of the house. He paused at the woodpile and carefully chose a stick of stovewood, a quartered, wedge-shaped piece. Armed with this he made for the woods. He did not notice the dawn-washed sky nor hear the trembling of the leaves in the fresh summer breeze. Jack Zachary felt weighed down with a black load of guilt wider than any sky.

In a secluded spot among the trees where the earth was still moist under the old leaves, he dug a trench and placed the stick in it with

34

the knife-sharp edge up. On this he knelt. "Oh, God, help me to find the answer," he prayed. Then, opening his prayer book and crossing himself, he began to repeat one prayer after another: "Holy Mary, Mother of God, pray for us now—" Over and over. On and on. He went to the seven prayers directed to the mortal wounds of Christ. "My sins have pierced your bleeding head. Have mercy on me."

The words burned into his soul and increased his guilt. Oh, to know, just to know that he was right with God! The pain caused by the knife-edged wood shot through his tortured knees and up through his body in lines of fire. Behind the prayers his thoughts kept pushing: "Take notice, God. I hope You're seeing what I'm suffering." Over and over he chanted the prayer forms until it seemed that the voice he heard was not his. Time dragged by. He caught himself beginning to slump. Fiercely he knelt erect again while pain engulfed him. "My sins have pierced your wounded hands. Blessed Saviour, have mercy on me."

His feet and legs became numb. A fire seemed to be burning at the back of his neck, and pain had become a way of life. But no assurance came, no peace.

"My sins have pierced your bleeding side. Blessed Saviour, have mercy—." His head swam. The green trees blurred before his eyes and wavered like reflections in water. Finally a merciful veil of darkness rose. Jack fell on his face.

When he finally opened his eyes, he couldn't remember what had happened. He could see that he had fallen into some low shrubs, but when he tried to get up, he found he could not move. Looking down, he saw his crumpled prayer book under him. Then he remembered.

He tried to turn his head, to move his hands, his feet, but his whole body seemed paralyzed. He tried to turn over. Again and again he tried. At last he lifted and turned his head enough to see the sky. Why, the sunlight was slanting from the west. That meant he had been lying there for several hours.

Long he gazed at the sky. "God! Where is this God? Here I am dying, and God doesn't care. What is it to Him? He didn't hear me. He didn't answer me. There is no heaven. Hell is a devilish invention. The whole thing is a tale. Well, I know now. It is just as good. I have finally discovered that we live in an empty universe."

Then he heard a sound—a bird singing. Jack couldn't turn to look for it, but the notes came closer as the bird flitted from branch to branch, scattering its silvery notes on the bleakness of Jack's mind. Suddenly, as though it knew perfectly well what it was about, the tiny creature lit on a branch just a few feet from Jack's face. Jack saw it clearly. Not a golden bird from paradise, but a common gray song sparrow. It sang with such fervor that the small feathered body fairly trembled. For several minutes it sang; then it flitted away.

"Why?" Jack wondered. "Why did this little fellow have to come and sing to me just when I've about convinced myself that the universe is meaningless? Someone must just be giving the orders to planet and tree and bird. Did that Someone care? But here I am dying. Why doesn't He do something?" He tried again to move, but to no avail. He tried to shout, to call for help, but no sound came, and he lay panting from the desperate effort.

Suddenly, clearly a question came to him. "But have you really been praying?" "No, no, I haven't," Jack admitted. "I don't communicate with people by set, memorized words. I have not been telling God my heart. Why shouldn't I talk to God directly?" Like a sunrise the dazzling thought came to him. "I will prove Him. I will just talk to Him." His thoughts clearly formed the words: "Oh, God, if You are in heaven, if Your Son is the Saviour of the world, please let me know that my sins are forgiven."

At once, right beside him, as if from a close companion, he heard a loving, authoritative voice: "Rise! Be My witness."

Immediately Jack bounded to his feet, the weakness and paralysis gone. He looked around. There, sticking out of the damp earth, was the buried stick; beside it the crumpled prayer book, and his cap. He picked up the cap, but felt no desire to retrieve the book, and he left it on the damp ground with the half-buried stick and the dead leaves.

Turning back through the woods, Jack cut across the meadow toward the house, all the time thinking, "This is my Father's world, my Father's universe." And over him the sky seemed to shine with a light that dimmed the very sun.

Once at the house, Jack strode into the kitchen. The man of the house, rocking in his favorite chair, turned to look at him in surprise just as the clock on the wall was striking four. "Why, Jack, where have you been? You didn't come to breakfast or dinner. We've been worried about you."

"Mr. Brown," the young man said, "I have had such food that I will never be hungry again, and drink that will satisfy my thirst as long as I live."

Mr. Brown seemed a little embarrassed. He changed the subject. "I've been walking through the fields," he said, "and it's so dry that if we don't get rain within the week, all our work will be for nothing. The young wheat is already turning yellow for lack of moisture."

"Do you believe in God?" Jack asked.

"Yes, of course," Mr. Brown replied.

Jack looked hard at his employer. "If you believed God was your Father, you would ask Him, and He would send rain."

"But God doesn't work that way, Jack. It is our responsibility to raise crops."

"Yes, but all the farmers in Canada cannot make one drop of rain."

Mr. Brown lifted his hand. "Listen, Jack, be reasonable. You see that barometer? The needle is on Fair. It's over as far as it can go. It is impossible for it to rain. There's no moisture in the air. It can't rain."

"Those are the most faithless words I've heard," Jack went on. "I know that God can make rain out of the dust if it pleases Him. For your sake I am going upstairs and ask Him, who has called me to be His witness, to send rain. Not tonight. Not tomorrow, but right now."

"There are no clouds." Mr. Brown frowned.

"God doesn't need clouds to send rain," Jack answered, and he headed up the stairs.

In his room he fell on his knees beside the bed, and in his heart he felt gratitude and a great peace as he thought of his sins, now forgiven.

Then for the second time in his life he talked to God. This time he spoke aloud. "Dear heavenly Father, not for my sake, for I know You have called me to be Your witness, but for the sake of Mr. Brown downstairs who doubts Your power, please send rain right now. Thank You! Thank You, heavenly Father."

Downstairs a door slammed, with a sharp report like the shot of a gun. Jack hurried down the stairs and, entering the kitchen, met Mr. Brown whose usually ruddy countenance had turned deathly pale. "It—it's going to rain," he faltered hoarsely.

And rain it did, in mighty torrents, with an overwhelming roar. The two men stood by the screen door gazing out in wonder, then spontaneously they embraced each other, laughing and crying at the same time.

"Thank You, God! Thank You, God!" Jack breathed.

The men went out on the porch to look around. There was not a sign of a cloud anywhere. The rain came straight from the clear sky, and the thirsty fields soaked up the water.

When the rest of the family returned in the car from young people's meeting at the church a few miles away they asked what had happened, for they had found the road as dusty as ever until they reached the borders of their property. There they found so much mud that they had to put chains on the tires to get through.

Mr. Brown told them of the miraculous rain, but Jack returned to his room to thank his heavenly Father.

As the family sat down to supper later, Mrs. Brown said, "Jack, I've been praying for you."

"Thank you," Jack said. "Your prayers have been answered."

Then Jack told of his agony the night before, of the torture in the woods, and of God's revelation to him. "Now," he said, "I know what I must do. I will be His witness to my people. They must have the pure gospel as it is revealed in the Bible."

"Amen," Mrs. Brown said, smiling at Jack. "Let's kneel and thank God." They all knelt in a glad prayer of consecration and thanksgiving.

A few days later while in the barn getting the horses out, Jack looked up to see a dignified stranger in a black suit coming into the barn. The stranger introduced himself as the Reverend Canton, pastor of the Methodist church.

"I have heard of your remarkable conversion," Pastor Canton began, "and I am here to extend to you the right hand of fellowship and to welcome you to our church."

"Thank you, sir," Jack said, raising his hand. "God asked me to be His witness, but as to the joining of a church, He never said anything;

38

therefore I am just going to do my job and wait until He tells me to join a church. And of course He will tell me what church to join. I have already found in the Holy Scriptures that God will have a special church in the last days. It says something about the church keeping the commandments and having the faith of Jesus. I don't understand as yet, but I am sure that God will reveal to me His true church on earth."

The minister cleared his throat to speak, but Jack went right on.

"There are so many churches, many teaching their own tradition rather than the doctrines of Jesus. How do I know that your church is not doing the same?"

"My boy," the minister replied, "we teach the Bible, and the Bible tells us not to forsake the assembling of the saints."

"Sir, I will have to find out who the saints are. I will not jump into joining any group until I am sure it is God's church on earth. I must find it. But I'll tell you what I will do; I'll visit your church, and if God shows me from His Book that it is the right church and that He wants me to become a member, I will."

With that, Pastor Canton left.

5

That Shineth More and More

Now that Jack had heard the call to be a "witness" for God, he wanted no material interests to bind him to earth. He decided to turn his share of the farm near Moline over to his brothers John and Alex. John and his wife-to-be would be glad for the extra land. Jack went to an attorney and deeded it officially. For a wedding gift he also gave them most of his earnings from his work at the Browns' farm, saving out just enough to pay his train fare to Saskatchewan. His book *Bible Readings* he took with him, and a few belongings. He began to search for God's true church and to study systematically. As he became convinced of a point, from that time on he followed it.

In Bromley, Saskatchewan, Jack took a job on a wheat farm with a family named Broughton. At the Broughtons', and wherever he went, he told of his wonderful heavenly Father and of the true church that God would one day show him.

All summer and fall Jack studied at every chance he got to sit and read. Then he felt a burden to go back to his parents' farm at Sandy Lake and share the knowledge of his new-found faith with them. Surely his parents would be happy to know God's will.

The first Sunday at home his mother begged him to go to church with her, for he had not attended since he and his brothers had moved onto the new farm across the river. To please his mother Jack consented to go to the early mass. After the mass certain of the members remained at the church. Since Jack's mother wanted to stay, he stayed with her and watched as each member produced large beeswax candles. He noted that some candles were larger than others. The size seemed to be determined by the wealth or generosity of the member. While the priest chanted a ritual, the candles were lighted. The room soon became stifling, with so many candles burning in the church and the doors and windows closed. Jack could hardly wait for the service to be over so that he could get out into the fresh air.

"What's this candle service all about?" he asked his mother as they started home.

"Oh, that is to let our light shine," she said. "Those who light the candles are called Brothers and Sisters."

"But, Mother, why do they do that when the sun is shining, giving all the light necessary?"

"Well, the sun shines, it is true; but Christ said, 'Let your light shine.'"

"Let your light shine! You pay for those huge candles and light them in the church in the daytime?" Jack protested.

"Didn't our blessed Saviour say that?" Mother Zachary looked at her son.

"Yes, Mother, but somebody stopped in the middle of His saying. Christ said, 'Let your light so shine before men, that they may see your good works, and glorify your Father which is in heaven.'"

They walked on, both deep in thought. At home Mother laid off her shawl and sat down awhile before preparing dinner. Father, who had been following behind, talking with neighbors, came in soon after.

"What do you think?" Mother Zachary turned to him. "Jack asked about the candles in the church. The church gets so hot and stuffy and that causes so many headaches. There are over 300 candles, all lighted at the same time. Why do we have those candles?"

Father slowly folded his hands behind his back. "I don't know if there is any real reason. We do many things in the church for no real reason. I guess somebody is just making good business selling all those candles."

Mother clucked her disapproval. "I'm sure I heard Father Keluznyatsky say it was to let our light shine because the blessed—"

"Yes, yes," Jack broke in, "and I told you the rest of the verse." He took his Bible which he always kept near, and found the verse, showing it to his father.

Helyar Zachary read the verse slowly. "It seems clear that Christ did not mean for us to purchase a candle and light it," he said. "A candle we should use to help someone in darkness. It is certainly of no value at midday. On the contrary, it is really harmful when there is no ventilation. Many times I leave church with a splitting headache."

"That is also my experience." Mother nodded. "Every time the windows are closed I get also a headache."

"You know," Father said, looking down at the Bible in his hand, "there may be other teachings of the church which do not follow the Holy Scriptures. That may be why the priest says that unauthorized people must not read the Scriptures."

"How is a person authorized?" Mother Zachary wanted to know.

"Through ordination," Father continued.

"But," Jack interrupted, "here in the Scriptures our Lord said, 'Search the Scriptures.' That is without qualification. It certainly would not be fair for the reading and interpreting of the Word of God to be left to one person. We all need to read and understand it. We all need salvation. Christ said that whosoever will may come. That invitation is to all; so all are responsible, not to the church or the priest, but to God. He alone knows who are ready to live in heaven, so He alone has the right to decide man's destiny." Jack reached for his Bible and, turning to Matthew 15, read, "'But in vain they do worship Me, teaching for doctrines the commandments of men.'"

"We can follow what the priests teach," Father Zachary put in, "provided it is in harmony with the Holy Scriptures."

"True, but the only way we can know whether they are in harmony with the Holy Scriptures is to read the Bible for ourselves. God certainly didn't give us His Word and then forbid us to read it," Jack said.

"Well, I think we are agreed that we should study the Holy Scriptures." Father Zachary nodded at Jack and Mother. "We have both a Ukrainian New Testament and the English Bible. With these two Bibles and Jacob's book, perhaps we should study the way of salvation."

Each Sunday Mother still begged Jack to attend church services with the family, but he preferred to stay at home and study for himself.

Finally in mid-February on a special holy day, Jack agreed to attend the church once more. On this day the church celebrated John's baptism of Jesus. There would be special ceremonies and then the blessing of some lake or stream. Then the hundreds of waiting people would come forward to fill their jugs and bottles with holy water for the year.

Mass began at seven in the morning. After the service at the church the procession formed, led by the priest. Men carrying gold and purple flags divided the procession into small groups, and each flag bearer had a guard of four to six men carrying guns with blank shells. Slowly they made their way to the lake a quarter of a mile from the church.

Jack shivered in the cold as he walked bareheaded with the other men. A biting wind nipped his ears. When the priest quickened his steps, Jack gladly followed suit.

At the lake they found that a hole had already been cut in the ice. The blocks of ice that had been removed were cut in the shape of crosses and decorated with colored tissue paper. The priest stepped onto the icy lake while the people huddled together on shore. He spoke some words of ritual and touched the water with his cross. The guardsmen fired their shots into the air. Then the people pressed forward to get their holy water.

Jack put on his cap quickly and turned to his mother, hoping to leave quickly.

"The priest will have dinner with us today." She smiled up at her son. "Come, we will walk along with him."

As they started toward home, Jack noticed that his father was not with them, but he assumed he was visiting with neighbors somewhere along the way. They stopped at the church and waited while the priest changed his robes; then they continued home. Jack opened the door of the house and there stood his father washing his dishes. He had already eaten!

"Heathen," the priest spat out, "eating without holy water."

"Indeed I did not eat without holy water," Helyar Zachary retorted. "I not only sprinkled the food, but I had a good drink of holy water."

"Where did you get your holy water?" the priest demanded.

"At the lake where you got yours."

"Are you a jackrabbit that you could run that fast and get here and have dinner already?" The priest glared at Helyar.

"I am no jackrabbit." Jack noted a twinkle in his father's eye. "In fact, I'm not as young as I once was, and I walked rather slowly."

"Well, where did you get the water?" the priest demanded.

"This morning I took a bottle with me to church, and after mass when you and the people went to the lake, I started home. I stopped at Novalkowski's place near the lake where there is a hole in the ice. I waited by the hole until I heard the shots fired. Then I knew the water was holy. I crossed myself, took a good drink of holy water, filled my bottle, and came home." Helyar Zachary shrugged his shoulders.

"That is not holy water," the priest objected.

"But did you divide the water in the lake?" Helyar asked.

The priest shook his head and stammered something about getting too smart in your old age.

Just then Mother Zachary called the family to dinner. Since they had fasted all morning, everyone began to heap his plate with food. For a while no one spoke as they began to eat. Jack sat deep in thought. He toyed with his food as he went over the morning's happenings, and this business of the holy water.

After the priest had left, Jack found his father sitting by the window reading the Bible. He drew up a chair beside his father. "Well, what do you think of all this?" he asked.

The old man ran a gnarled hand through his white shock of hair. "Jacob, I tell you the truth. I am really troubled. When I was a boy going to school in the old country, the priest used to come and teach us the catechism. I remember once he said, 'Children, you must do what I tell you, but it is not necessary to do what I do.' But now I don't believe it is even safe to do what they tell us."

"No, I don't either," Jack agreed. "What do you think of this making of holy water?"

"As a matter of fact," Father said, "I have been reading in your Bible the account of creation. At the end of each day God said, 'It is good.' Now goodness and holiness seem to me to be much the same thing. If God made the water good, why do priests have to make it holy? It doesn't make sense to me." Father shook his head.

"We will study more," Jack promised. "There are many things

44

to learn." Jack's heart felt light. His mother and father both seemed anxious to know the truth. Now if he could only interest his young friends—

Jack, Alex, and their sister Mary had always attended the community dance every Saturday night, although Jack never danced. But now that he had found his heavenly Father, Jack felt he could not invite Him to go into the place where the dance was held. The night of the dance Alex and Mary went with their own friends, and Jack took a horse and sleigh to call for a pretty, dark-eyed neighbor girl, Mary Restifanyuk. He drove her to the farm where the dance was being held, tied the horse, and walked with her to the door. "Well, Mary," he said, opening the door, "I will pick you up at midnight."

"Why, Jack! You mean you aren't coming in?" She turned to him.

He let the door close against the squeak and thump of the fiddlers. "No, I'm not coming in."

"Why not?" Mary asked. "Last summer I found a Friend," Jack began slowly, "and I've followed Him ever since. He just doesn't go to dances."

"What do you mean? I thought I was your friend."

"So you are, or I wouldn't have brought you here as a favor. But you are my earthly friend. He is my heavenly Friend."

"Who are you talking about?" Mary's voice rose.

"My Saviour," Jack answered quietly.

"Oh." The girl shrugged. "You're getting too religious."

"Have a good time; I'll pick you up at midnight." Jack opened the door again, and Mary went in without a word.

Jack looked at his watch. Eight-thirty! Where should he go until midnight? He had his Bible in a grocery bag in the sleigh, for it was too large for his pocket. Why, he could call on nearby neighbors and offer to study with them, he decided.

At the first home the neighbors were not interested. At the next house, the man of the house invited him in, and Jack stayed to study the Bible until midnight, when he left to get Mary.

The dance had just ended when Jack arrived. She walked with him to the sleigh and he helped her in, placing the buffalo robe across her lap. Then he climbed in beside her and, taking the reins, clucked a giddap to the horse. Jack tried to pick up the conversation where they had left off earlier in the evening, but Mary spoke little and held herself aloof on her side of the sleigh.

"It isn't safe, Mary," Jack said at last, "to go where one could not take the Saviour with him, and I am sure He would not go into a dance hall."

He felt her eyes upon him and a strange feeling came over him as he turned toward her.

"Are you going to be a priest or monk?" Mary asked softly.

"No, indeed. But I want to be a child of God and live with Him through ages and ages."

"But—but the priest is responsible for all of us," Mary protested. "We pay them to pray for us all the time."

"Oh, Mary, don't be deceived in such important matters. Priests have enough of their own sins to look after. We are responsible to God ourselves for the characters we develop."

Jack heard Mary sigh, and she turned away from him as he drove up the road to her house. "Promise me you'll think about these things. Please, Mary?" Jack begged.

Mary gave a nervous laugh as she alighted from the sleigh. Then with a quick Thanks and Good-bye, she hurried into the house. For a moment he sat in the sleigh staring at the house into which Mary had gone and slammed the door.

Although Jack phoned her several times after that and met her often in town, and tried to talk to her about giving her life to Christ, Mary always shrugged away the invitation. "That is the priest's responsibility," she'd say with a laugh.

6

Running From God

The following spring Jack left Sandy Lake and went to his brother John's farm near Moline—the place they had purchased from Adam Croft. He knew his brother would be pleased to have help with his spring planting; and besides, people around Sandy Lake were beginning to suspect him of heresy.

In Moline he enjoyed visiting Mr. Croft, a Lutheran. Every Sunday the two men visited some Protestant church. They also studied the Bible together, and Jack never wearied of hearing the older man tell stories of Martin Luther, that fearless man of God. Jack felt a great identity with Luther. He took courage from Luther's boldness and from his fearless stand against the selling of indulgences. Later on, the memory of Luther's unyielding faith strengthened Jack to stand firmly through tests that came to him.

One hot summer day late in July while the family sat around the dinner table, Jack looked out the window to see Adam Croft's Chevrolet rattling up the lane. He excused himself and went out to meet his friend.

"Jack," Mr. Croft announced, jumping out of the car, "I have a young man with me who is the answer to your prayers. He knows more about the Bible and God's plan for His people than all these churches I've been taking you to."

Jack noticed the young stranger in the car. "Why, he's scarcely more than a boy," Jack thought. "Come into the house," he urged, leading the way.

Mr. Croft introduced the young man, Jack Webb, a senior from Maplewood Academy in Hutchinson, Minnesota. "He's selling books to earn a scholarship for the next school year," Mr. Croft finished.

"I'm selling the wonderful book, *Our Day in the Light of*

Prophecy," Mr. Webb said. "If you're a Bible student, I know you'll enjoy it."

Suddenly Jack had an idea. "Say, friend, if you're so good with the Bible and know God's plan so well, tell me how can I get in touch with the people who put out a book I have. If you can tell me that, I'll buy every book you've got." Jack left the room and soon returned with his Bible Readings.

"Why," the salesman exclaimed, "that's our book!"

"What do you mean?" Jack asked. "What I mean is, that I represent the Review and Herald Publishing Association, the publisher of that book." He pulled from his pocket a black order pad stamped in gold with the name, "Review and Herald Publishing Association."

"That's proof enough," Jack said. "What other books do you have—the ones under your arm there?"

"Well, these are little paperbound books." Mr. Webb handed several to Jack.

"*The Second Coming of Christ, The Vatican and the War, The Christian Sabbath, The Other Side of Death.*" Jack read the titles. "How much are they by the dozen?"

That day, before the colporteur left, Jack bought *Our Day in the Light of Prophecy,* and all the paperbound books the other young man had, as well as subscribing to the *Review and Herald, The Youth's Instructor,* and *The Watchman.* After the young man left, Jack spent every possible moment with his books, and he eagerly watched the mail for his magazines to come.

And then one afternoon in early August when Jack had finished raking hay and was leading the horses toward the barn and the watering trough, he saw a strange bicycle by the front door, and over by the watering trough his sister-in-law, Annie, vigorously pumping water for the horses.

Must be something wrong, Jack said to himself as he came up to Annie and saw the smoldering glance she shot at him.

"Serves you right," she snapped. "You're so in love with that book. You almost worship it. And now what do you think?"

"What's the matter, Annie? What's wrong with the book?"

"The same thing I always tell you. It's not for us!"

"What? Why not for us?" Jack asked.

Her voice dropped to a whisper as she answered, "Do you know who those people are? The ones that sell your precious books? They are all Jews, the same Jews who killed our blessed Lord. And their representative is in the house right now."

Jack's face broke into a smile. "Why, Annie, what a privilege we will have to straighten out these poor mixed-up Jews! How thankful we should be to have a Jew in our house tonight! God must have sent him to get straightened out."

Annie seemed to calm down a little at Jack's words. "You'd better be careful," she cautioned. "He's very quiet, but he's tricky. Don't be so sure of him."

Jack went into the house to meet the visitor. Ojala was his name. And, as Annie had said, he was quiet and soft-spoken. Now with Ukrainian hospitality Jack invited the man to stay for supper. Annie busied herself with preparations for the evening meal, wondering when the man would begin to talk religion. Steaming plates of fresh corn, green beans, mashed potatoes, green onions, eggs, as well as a large platter of pork chops were placed on the table, and Jack, John, Annie, and their guest began to eat.

Annie picked up the platter of pork chops. "Jack is funny. He doesn't eat meat. Doesn't believe in killing anything. Help yourself," she said, handing the platter to the visitor.

The stranger smiled and passed the platter on to John without taking any himself. All through the meal Annie and Jack waited for the man to bring up religion. But not one word did he say about it.

By the time supper ended, Jack could hardly contain himself. Was the man a Jew or what? Finally he turned to him and said, "Sir, is it not a blessing to know that Christ Jesus came to seek and save the lost, and that salvation is only through Him?"

"Amen," the guest answered. "Indeed that is the foundation of Christian faith."

Jack looked at the man sharply. "Is it possible to be saved or get to heaven any other way?" he continued.

With a big smile the visitor said, "No, indeed not. Christ said, 'I am the way, the truth, and the life! no man cometh unto the Father, but by Me.'"

"Mr. Ojala," Annie spoke up, "didn't you say something about Saturday being holy, not Sunday?"

Jack looked from Annie to Mr. Ojala. "What's this about Saturday being holy?"

Opening his Bible, the visitor turned to the second chapter of Genesis. Jack quickly got out his Bible and followed along.

"'And God blessed the seventh day, and sanctified it,'" Mr. Ojala read aloud: "'because that in it He had rested from all His work which God created and made.'"

"Of course the seventh day is holy. I keep it every week," Jack agreed.

"But the holy day you call the seventh," protested Mr. Ojala, "is not the seventh, but the first. We start the week with the first day and end with the seventh. That's the way it is still recorded on the calendars."

"Not on my calendar, it isn't." Jack shook his head.

Mr. Ojala walked over to the large calendar that hung on the wall and pointed out the order of the days of the week, while Jack stared.

Sure enough. Each week began with Sunday and ended with Saturday, the seventh day of the week. Jack shook his head as if trying to awaken himself. "I am hypnotized," he thought. "Surely I couldn't have been so blind all my life." He ran to his room where he had a calendar that Mr. Ojala had never seen, but to his surprise, it was exactly the same as the one in the kitchen. Quietly he returned and slumped down into a chair. The big calendar on the wall mocked him. Then it seemed that from a long way off he heard Mr. Ojala speaking to him.

"Brother Zachary, tell me how you came to have the book *Bible Readings*."

Jack straightened up. He loved to tell of the auction sale that had changed his life, and of the day in the woods when God had called him to be His witness.

"A very remarkable experience," said Mr. Ojala when Jack had finished. "God has called you to do a work for Him; I am sure of that. For weeks the brethren at the Manitoba Conference office in

50

Winnipeg have been having special prayer that God would provide a worker for the Ukrainian people in the Manitoba territory. One fifth of the population in this province are Ukrainian, you know. Well, when Brother Webb sent in his report about meeting you and about your having bought all his books, the conference sent me here to Moline to investigate the interest of one Jack Zachary. I was under the impression that you already knew about the Sabbath. I noticed the shocked look on your sister-in-law's face when I mentioned the seventh-day Sabbath when I first arrived, and I realized you had not yet heard about it."

The men talked on and on. The hour grew late, and Jack finally led the visitor to his own room, where they sat for some time studying quietly.

"Another thing that most people have confused," Mr. Ojala said, "is the measurement of time. According to Bible reckoning, as we can read in Genesis 1 and Leviticus 23:32, each twenty-four-hour day begins at sunset, but man reckons from midnight to midnight. This is man's reckoning, not God's."

Jack listened in a daze. Though everything the man said was from the Bible, it was completely new to him. "You see, it was man who changed the day of worship, not God," Mr. Ojala went on. "We read in Daniel 7:25 the prophecy of the change of time by the man of sin." He explained clearly the identity of this power and said, "So you see, even the Protestants are paying homage to the papacy without knowing it."

"Please," Jack held up his hand to stop Mr. Ojala, I need time to think. Will you write out for me a few texts that prove the seventh-day Sabbath is the Christian Sabbath? I must study them later."

The visitor wrote out the references and handed the paper to Jack.

"Thank you, friend. I will study these carefully." He folded the paper and put it in his overalls pocket.

"The hour is late," Mr. Ojala finally said, closing his Bible. "We must go to bed. Unfortunately I must return to Winnipeg in the morning."

As soon as Mr. Ojala had left for Winnipeg, Jack, his mind in a whirl, made some hurried plans. Here, he had visited churches so carefully, trying to keep his mind clear of error, trying to find God's

51

church. Now this queer, part Jewish, part Christian religion which he had never heard of before seemed to be entangling him. He had to think this through carefully. He would go back to the Broughtons' in Saskatchewan where he had worked the summer before. Perhaps they could help him straighten out his tangled feelings. Without telling John and Annie where he was going, Jack left by train for Bromley, Saskatchewan.

Catholics he could handle, and some Protestants, but these mixed-up Christian-Jews——well, their arguments were too big.

Jack arrived at the Broughtons' while they were busy harvesting. Since he had already proved his faithfulness and skill in running the threshing machines, they welcomed him gladly. Mrs. Broughton, knowing that Jack didn't eat meat, always made sure he had eggs and vegetables, even sending special food to him at noon when he threshed for neighbors some miles away.

Once during his stay Jack decided to write to John and Annie back in Manitoba, but fearing those Christian Jews from Winnipeg might trace him, he arranged to have the letter mailed from Kisbey, several miles from Bromley.

And sure enough, when Mr. Ojala, back at the conference office in Winnipeg, had reported on his visit to Jack Zachary, they sent him back to Moline to contact Jack again.

"He ran like a jackrabbit," Annie said, meeting Mr. Ojala at the door. "Guess you scared him away."

"I'm very sorry to hear that," the man said. "Have you had any word from him?"

Annie showed him the letter postmarked Kisbey, Saskatchewan.

Mr. Ojala wrote down that much and left. Once more he reported to the conference officials in Winnipeg, who kept praying for Jack. They felt sure that God had called him to work for his people, for Brother Ojala had told them Jack's story.

Although he had never met Jack, George Soper, the head of the Tract Society, decided to write. He mailed the letter to Kisbey, Saskatchewan, with a prayer that God would guide it to its destination.

It was on a Saturday evening in October, when the threshing was finished and Jack was wondering what should be his next move, that

Mr. Broughton came home with a letter for him. It had arrived at Kisbey, and would have been returned to Winnipeg except that the postmaster mentioned in the presence of his daughter that he had a letter for some fellow "Zachary."

"Oh, Dad, that's that boy at Broughtons' who's so full of religion," she said. So the postmaster forwarded the letter to Bromley in care of Mr. Broughton.

Jack tore open the envelope and drew out the neatly typed letter.

Dear Brother Zachary:

God has called you to be His witness, but like Jonah you are running away.

There was more, but that first sentence hit home. He went up to his room and paced the floor. Then with his hands stuffed in his overalls pocket, he felt a piece of stiff folded paper. He drew it out and noticed that the edges were torn; but as he smoothed it out, he found every one of the texts written down by Mr. Ojala.

Jack sat down and began to study the texts. As he read text after text, rays of light seemed to illumine his mind. In the brightening light he traced the Sabbath from its beginning in Eden before Jews existed, through the law at Sinai, through Christ's time, to the restored earth. He read Isaiah 66:22, 23 over and over. "From one Sabbath to another, shall all flesh come to worship before Me, saith the Lord." Before he slept that night, Jack Zachary knew for a certainty that the seventh day is God's eternal Sabbath for all men. He would keep the Sabbath holy. That night he fell asleep with a feeling of great peace in his heart.

Early the next morning Jack awoke before the rest of the family. He dressed and went out to saddle the pony; then he went out to look for the cows. Jack soon had them rounded up and headed for the barn. The field he had to cross edged a small lake which had receded, leaving a pile of stones and larger rocks in the hayfield.

Those stones would be in the way when it came time for haying, Jack thought to himself, and stopped his pony. Everything looked so peaceful; a breeze rippled through the long prairie grass. Beyond, the vast fields with their stubble rows ran on and on to the horizon. Jack noticed the stillness. Of course, it was Sunday. Any other day by this time the air would be full of the rattle of machines and the calls of workmen. Why is it, he thought, that man says, "Keep the first day," and everybody obeys? God says, "Keep the seventh day," and everybody works?

Jack jumped quickly off his pony and headed for the rock pile.

Those rocks too big to lift, he rolled or dragged into the pond. He got wet and muddy, but he not only removed the obstructing rocks, he also showed to whom he had pledged his allegiance.

When he had cleared away the rocks, he gathered the cows again, drove them into the barn, and turned the pony loose in the pasture. No one seemed to be up at the house yet, he noted. He might as well cut the wood by the shed. Picking up the ax, he began making the chips fly as the ringing chop of his blade echoed through the still air.

A little later Mrs. Broughton came out of the house carrying a pail on her way to the barn to milk the cows. She stopped when she saw Jack chopping wood. "Why, Jack, don't you know this is Sunday?"

"Yes, ma'am, I do. But this is not God's holy day. This day is man made. I intend to obey God rather than man." The ax came down in another mighty swing.

Mrs. Broughton's shock showed on her face. "What's happened to your religion?"

"What's happened? I'm just finding my true religion."

"But—but, Jack, I don't understand. You were always so religious—"

"Mrs. Broughton," Jack leaned on the ax handle as the head rested on the chopping block, "Sunday has been the first day of the week since God made the weekly cycle at creation. The seventh day of the week is Saturday. Just look at your calendar. God has said, 'The seventh day is the Sabbath of the Lord thy God: in it thou shalt not do any work.' Man says, 'Rest the first day, then work six days, including Saturday.' Well, Mrs. Broughton, I will obey God from now on."

Early Wednesday morning of that week Jack decided to return to his brother's place in Moline. "Surely," he thought, "if I explain about the seventh day to John and Annie, they will keep the Sabbath with me."

7

Meet Me in the New Earth

Jack told the Broughtons of his plan to leave that day so that he would be back in Moline before the weekend. Mr. Broughton promised to drive him to the station at Kennedy that evening where Jack hoped to get the fast train. He would have part of Thursday and all day Friday to tell John and Annie about the Sabbath!

"Here's your wages and five dollars extra," Mr. Broughton said. "We hate to lose you. Thanks to you, we made a good record in harvesting this year. You kept the machinery going all the time. Come back next season."

They drove to the station, where the two men gripped hands before parting. "Remember the welcome is always out for you, my boy." Mr. Broughton smiled as he started up the old car and headed home, leaving Jack at the empty station.

When Jack could no longer see the taillights of the car going down the road, he went into the station waiting room. The dim light showed the pot-bellied stove in the center of the room, the empty ticket office across the room, several hard benches, and a spittoon. Jack remembered his feeling of loneliness and bewilderment when he had come to Saskatchewan not many weeks before. Then he had been running away from the Sabbath. But now he was going cheerfully to meet it.

According to the train schedule on the wall, the train would not come through until morning. Jack stretched out on one of the benches and dozed. The station agent, opening the ticket office in the morning, awoke him.

"I want a ticket to Moline, Manitoba," Jack told the agent.

"Well, young fella, you can't go straight to Moline from here. You will have to take the local and connect with the main line."

"When will I get to Moline?" Jack asked.

"Not until late tomorrow afternoon."

There was nothing to do but buy the ticket and wait. Jack slumped down on the bench in the corner. He had counted so much on having that extra day to tell John and Annie about the Sabbath. Now he would be fortunate if he arrived at the farm before the Sabbath began.

"Why! Why didn't God help me to get the better train?" he fretted.

At nine o'clock the morning local pulled into the station, and Jack boarded the train. It crept slowly out of the station and on down the tracks, never seeming to get up any speed, stopping continually for mail and freight and passengers. Jack looked around at his fellow passengers. Sitting across the aisle from him were a lady and a little girl. The child smiled at him and then confided, "I'm three years old." After a pause she went on, "How old are you?"

Jack smiled. Wealthy Americans, he thought, noticing the appearance of the little girl's mother and the expensive beaver coat hanging above the seat and the fine luggage on the rack above.

Just then the conductor came through the coach, and Jack, remembering he had not eaten since the day before, asked how long the train would stop at the next station.

"We take on water there," the conductor said. "You'll have time to get off the train and buy food." He passed on down the aisle and into the next coach.

"Oh, sir," the lady across the aisle turned to Jack with a smile, "would you be so kind as to buy a dozen oranges for my little girl if you are going to get off the train at the next station? Here is a dollar bill, and thank you very much."

Jack took the American bill and agreed to get the oranges at the next stop. Already the train was slowing down, so Jack hurried to the end of the coach and got off the train.

When he returned with the oranges, he handed the lady thirty-five cents in change.

"Oh, no," she said, "you keep the change for your trouble." When she refused the money after Jack urged it upon her, he went to his seat. He didn't like being paid for doing a simple good turn. He fingered the money. Thirty-five cents. Why, that was just what those little paperback books cost. He reached into his pocket and pulled one out. *The Vatican and the War*. He handed her the book with, "I'd like you to read this."

"Thank you," she said as she took the book. "But let me pay you for it."

Jack refused. He began to pray that God would use the book to touch her heart. Then from time to time he glanced covertly at her as she began to read the book. Jack thought, "She has such a lovely smile and a manner so becoming to a Christian." Then he prayed again. "Dear Lord, help her to see the truth."

Suddenly, as if she had found a venomous snake between the pages of the book, the lady cried, "Oh! You sly heretic! How dare you?" And she tossed the book across the aisle into Jack's seat.

Jack looked around, and his face reddened. The other people in the car had perked up their ears and leaned forward, to see what was happening.

"Oh, lady," Jack pleaded, "don't be angry. I'm sorry I hurt you. I never meant to do that. You're not a Catholic, are you?"

"A Catholic? I am a Catholic, and proud of it."

"Lady, please forgive me. I did not mean to upset you. But you see, I have been reading the Holy Scriptures, and I have learned many things."

The lady seemed to calm herself. She looked up at Jack. "I read the Holy Scriptures also," she said with dignity, "and from the Holy Scriptures the Catholics are right."

"Do you mean that all Catholic teaching is based on the Scriptures?" Jack asked.

"Of course. Of course it's based on the Scriptures."

"Lady, do you have a copy of the Holy Scriptures with you?"

She nodded. "I'll show you." From her bag she pulled out a Douay version and began leafing through it. "Christ said, 'Peter, I build My church upon you, and you will take My place on earth.'" Finally she looked up at Jack. "Haven't you read that in your Bible?"

59

Jack was searching in his own Bible. After several minutes, during which neither of them could find the verse, Jack's eyes fell on John 3:16. "You believe that people will go to heaven or hell, don't you? Please read aloud John 3:16."

The lady read aloud, "'For God so loved the world, that He gave His only-begotten Son, that whosoever believeth in Him should not perish—'"

"Wait," Jack held up his hand. "Do you believe in hellfire that burns without ending?"

"Well, yes—"

"But what did you just read? '...should not perish.' What does 'perish' mean?"

"Well, uh, it means to die, to-uh-to stop existing, I suppose."

"Exactly. To stop living. But the church says the sinner will live for eternity in tormenting fire. The Holy Scriptures say they will cease to exist. Who is right?"

"But somewhere I know it says the sinner will burn with everlasting fire." The lady seemed puzzled.

"Those expressions have been misunderstood, madam. Read Jude 7. Notice what it says: 'Sodom and Gomrrah...are set forth for an example, suffering the vengeance of eternal fire.' These cities are not still burning. Yet they suffered eternal fire. The effect of the fire is eternal. So it will be with all sinners who suffer the vengeance of eternal fire."

The lady wore an expression of perplexity mixed with wonder, but she said nothing; so Jack continued: "There are many such errors in the teachings of the church. Here is another one. Notice Matthew 28, verses 18 and 19, 'Go ye therefore, and teach all nations, baptizing them—' Catholics baptize first and then teach. Christ said, 'Go and teach,' and after they have accepted the way of life, baptize them. Baptism is a public testimony that a person is buried with Christ. He must be immersed. How can he live a new life if he is not resurrected by God's Spirit as Christ was resurrected? It is not fair to take a child and sprinkle water on it, call it a child of God, and then teach it contrary to Christ's teachings. I presume your child was baptized?"

The lady nodded.

"But she doesn't remember," he continued. "What good did it do her? Your duty is to teach her what Christ taught, and when she accepts Him as her Saviour, then she can be baptized into His death and resurrection."

Jack paused for a moment; then he went on, "If we obey man, we can look only for a reward given by men. But Christ is able to reward His faithful ones. He said, 'In my Father's house are many mansions....I go to prepare a place for you.' God alone admits people to heaven."

Now Jack became so engrossed in telling the lady of the way of life that he forgot all about the other passengers watching and straining to hear the conversation. He didn't notice when the train slowed down for the stop at Brandon, the railway terminal.

Just before reaching the terminal the train jerked to a stop, and the lady began hurriedly to gather her things together. Jack stepped back to his seat to get his coat when he heard the little girl speak to her mother.

"Don't cry, Mommy! Please don't cry!"

Jack looked over at the mother. She was fumbling for something in her handbag. There were tears on her cheeks. At last she pulled a lace-edged handkerchief from her bag and wiped her eyes.

"Madam," Jack spoke softly, "the Holy Scriptures say, 'The truth shall make you free.' Have you asked your Saviour who shed His blood for you to take away your sins?"

The lady shook her head as the tears continued to flow.

The train started up again, slowly grinding along to the terminal.

"No better time than now to accept your Saviour's sacrifice and invitation," Jack went on.

"I want to do that," she whispered.

Quickly Jack moved across the aisle, knowing he had but a few more moments left. "Let's bow our heads and pray," he suggested. "Dear Lord," he began, "please accept me as I am. I want Jesus to be my personal Saviour. Amen."

The lady now smiled at Jack as she put on her coat. "By the way, what church do you belong to?" she asked.

"To tell you the truth, I have not found the name of the true church, but I am looking for it. The remnant, or last church on earth, will keep all the Ten Commandments including the fourth, which tells us which day to keep. The Sabbath is not Sunday. Sunday was set apart as a holy day not by God but by the church fathers. You can read that in any Catholic book on doctrines. God's people keep the seventh-day Sabbath, which is Saturday, set aside by Christ at creation."

The train had made its final stop, and the passengers were crowding the aisles. "Come," Jack said, picking up the baggage, "I will help you." And he led the way out of the train.

They stood on the station platform with the crowd milling around them. "Be faithful," Jack said, holding out his hand. "I make an appointment to meet you in the earth made new. I want you for a neighbor there."

The lady looked up into Jack's eager countenance. "I will look for you, dear friend."

As Jack watched the lady and her little girl walk away, the thought came to him, "So this is why I missed connections and had to take the local train? Yes, all things work together for good."

8

Disowned

When Jack arrived at his brother's farm, it was almost sundown. Annie had begun to prepare supper; but after their greeting Jack suggested that she and John have worship with him. Jack turned the pages in his Bible to the fifteenth chapter of John. Then he began to read: "'I am the vine, ye are the branches: he that abideth in Me, and I in him, the same bringeth forth much fruit: for without Me ye can do nothing....Ye are My friends, if ye do whatsoever I command you....The servant is not greater than his lord. If they have persecuted Me, they will also persecute you.'" He closed the Bible and knelt to pray. He prayed that they all might have courage and determination to obey God even as Christ obeyed His Father and never failed. The prayer over, Jack began to talk before Annie went back to the meal preparation.

"Do you know," he said, "that the whole world is wrong, with the exception of a few loyal people who believe in the Lord Jesus and keep the Ten Commandments according to His Word?" Annie and John looked surprised at Jack's words. Then Jack saw Annie shrug her shoulders.

Undaunted, Jack opened his Bible as well as a catechism he always carried with him and began to compare the Ten Commandments as written in both. "You see," he said, his finger on the second commandment in the Bible, "the church has taken out that commandment altogether. But no man has the right to tamper with God's Word. It was also the church which told men long ago in the fourth century at the Council of Laodicea, to worship God on Sunday instead of on Saturday. And you know in our Ukrainian language the only name for the seventh day is Subota, which means Sabbath."

Annie turned on Jack. "They did get you, didn't they?" She gave him a withering look.

"Who got me?"

"Why, those people, those Jews," Annie's voice rose. "That man that was here."

"No, indeed," Jack answered. "No one got me. Only the Holy Spirit got me. I am going to obey God regardless of the cost."

"Jack, I'm surprised at you," Annie went on. "Thousands of much smarter people than you all keep Sunday just as their parents have done for years."

"Annie, in the past there have been smart, wise people who pointed out the errors of the church and stood firm, but they were silenced by fires. Such men as Huss and Jerome and thousands of others were burned for their beliefs."

"Well," retorted Annie, "I still think the priests are responsible. They taught us what they liked. It's not our fault if we're ignorant. Anyway, you and John can talk religion all night, if you like. I'm going to get supper." And with this, she flounced back to the stove to fry the potatoes.

Sabbath morning early, Jack rushed over to see Adam Croft and talk to him about the commandments, especially the fourth.

"I don't see," said Croft, "why it matters which day we keep, as long as we keep one."

"But why did God make it so specific?" persisted Jack. "He said, 'Remember the seventh day,' not a seventh day."

"Now, Jack, you'd better be careful. You know Paul said we can't earn our way to heaven by keeping the law."

"True enough," Jack answered, "but we certainly will lose heaven if we don't keep it. The Ten Commandments are the standard of the judgment."

But Mr. Croft shook his head. "I don't think it is that important," he said.

Jack felt frustrated. True, his brother John hadn't said much, but Annie volubly rejected all that was not blessed by the priest; Adam Croft simply couldn't see the importance of keeping all the commandments; and there were still his parents to face. How could people be so blind? Why couldn't they see what was so clear and beautiful to him?

A few days later Jack started for Sandy Lake, where his parents still lived. He hoped to be there in plenty of time to keep his second Sabbath with his folks. When he arrived at the gate and started up the path to the house, he saw his mother coming to meet him. "Oh, Jack," she wailed, "how dare you disgrace me like this?"

Jack put his arm around her shoulder. "Mother, I love you. I'm sorry."

"Sure, that's what Judas said when he betrayed Christ," his mother sobbed. Jack swallowed the lump in his throat but could not answer. They went into the house. Now the meaning of Christ's words, "Ye shall be hated of all men for My name's sake," was beginning to be clear.

Jack soon learned why his mother was so upset. The whole community, she said, was talking about her son Jacob becoming a Jew and preaching to everybody that Christ was not the Messiah. "It is a terrible disgrace," she sobbed, wringing her hands.

On Sunday, Mother Zachary begged Jack to go to church with her. "Perhaps the people, seeing you at church, will be kinder in their judgment," she reasoned. And Jack, not wishing to hurt her more, finally consented to go.

Mass proceeded as usual, followed by the sermon. The priest stood looking over the congregation; then he began to speak: "My heart aches to bring you terrible news," he began. "I wish it was about someone else. No doubt some of you already know that one of our most trusted sheep has gone astray. He is bent on destroying the church of God on earth. When a murderer takes physical life, his penalty is death, but here is an even greater offense. Heretics destroy souls, which are of much greater value than physical life. Therefore, anyone who eliminates heretics from society brings honor to the church and glory to God. I now proclaim that this young man is a heretic and excommunicated from our Catholic community. Anyone who harbors this heretic will receive the same condemnation."

A great buzz and murmuring arose in the congregation, and Jack noticed many hostile eyes turned to stare at him. Since the women and men sat on separate sides in the Ukrainian church, Jack glanced across to the women's side at his mother, her face red and tear-stained. How he longed to comfort her, but he must not publicly expose her as the mother of a heretic. Under the hard eyes of his former friends, he edged his way to the door and fled.

The clean, cold air felt good on his face. Briskly he walked along the frozen road, and once again the words of Jesus comforted him: "If they have persecuted Me, they will also persecute you." As he thought of all humankind he had ever known, he could think of no one to whom he could turn at that moment. No one but God. "Oh, Father, give me strength to stand firmly for Your truth," he prayed.

Arriving home, he entered the empty house and looked around at the familiar objects—the homely square stove, gleaming with polish; the table with its hand-crocheted tablecloth put on for Sunday; the familiar shrine of Mary in the corner; the picture of Christ, His heart encircled with thorns. How strangely foreign everything looked. His glance wandered to the sideboard and the delicious *kalachi* or coffee cake his mother always made for Sunday, but he was not hungry. Not wanting to be there when the family returned from church, he went out and followed the road to the lake. The wind stung his face as he walked slowly along the deserted trail.

What would his father do? Of course there was but one answer. His father would have to disown him to keep his standing in the community and in the church. Jack watched the dark water lapping at the clear thin ice that edged the shore, sharp, cutting, cold. On and on he walked, all unconscious of the passing time.

As he turned to walk back along the lake, across the road, and up to the house, darkness settled. His father stood at the door waiting for him. "Jack," his voice sounded stern, "this is your own choice, to separate yourself from society and from the church; and now in order to remain in favor with the church, we will have to disown you."

Jack knew there was little to say. "I will always love you and pray for you," he said quietly. "I know your position in the community."

Mother Zachary came into the kitchen, her face swollen with weeping. "Here is a letter for you, Jack. It was brought out to the house this afternoon." Quickly he opened the official-looking envelope. "Well," he said, glancing through the letter, "I guess my new home will be the army. I almost forgot, but Canada is at war in Europe. And there is no time to lose. According to the dates in the letter, I am already two days late."

The next morning found him on the train, bound for Winnipeg—and the army. Silently he watched the bleak, dun-colored landscape pass. As the train emerged from a stand of birch trees, he could see in the distance his father's house with a plume of smoke drifting from the chimney. Tears stung his eyes. Would he ever see his home again?

9

A Good Soldier of Jesus

The train arrived in Winnipeg in the late afternoon, and Jack reported immediately to the Minto Street Barracks. There were the usual forms to fill out, and at one point the clerk asked him about his religious affiliations.

"I don't belong to any church right now," Jack answered. "I am looking for a church which I will join as soon as I find it."

"But I have to have the name of a church. What church were you christened into?"

"That has nothing to do with what I believe now. I have severed all connections with that church."

"But what will I put here?" insisted the clerk pointing at the form.

"Put down Protestant."

Jack moved on to the next station. Here they gave him a kit of supplies and a bedroll, and sent him to the barracks where he was assigned a cot space. After supper in the mess hall he returned to the barracks, a huge noisy hall, filled with soldiers getting settled in after a week of field training. Jack carefully put his things in order and then settled down to read his New Testament. Just before ten o'clock when the main lights would be turned out for the night, Jack knelt to pray by his mat.

"Whaddya know, boys? We got a prophet," someone in the barracks yelled.

"I bet he's a false prophet," a sneering voice answered.

"Yeah. Let's stone him." And the boots began to fly amid shouts, curses, and loud laughs. The heavy boots, reinforced with steel, hit

Jack on all sides. He buried his face to keep from being scarred, but the boots hit his ears, his head, his hands. When the barrage stopped he raised his head, blood streaming down his face and into his eyes. There were boots piled all around him. Then the boys, jeering and laughing, came up asking for their property. As Jack, half blinded by blood, handed over each boot, some fellow would be sure to say, "This is not mine. You're a false prophet." Then would follow a stream of curses. At last the men settled down, and Jack made his way to the washroom. He washed the blood from his hands and face. It took some time to comb his hair, so matted had it become with blood. But he was thankful he had not been seriously hurt. "Dear Jesus," he prayed, "You were cut and bruised for me. Give me the courage to pray tomorrow night, no matter what the cost, like Daniel in Babylon."

The next night about a half hour before lights out, one of the two colored boys in the battalion came over to Jack. "Say, I am also a Christian, and I have come to ask your forgiveness. I did not throw any boots last night, but I stood and watched when I should have helped you. I didn't have courage enough to perform my Christian duty."

Jack smiled at his unexpected new companion. "When the lights go out, let us both kneel down in prayer before God, and if they throw boots, they throw boots." Jack shrugged. "It doesn't hurt as much as you might think."

As soon as the lights dimmed for the night and the two boys knelt in prayer side by side, the shouts went up. "Look. We got two false prophets. Let's stone 'em before they make more." But that night only a few of the boys threw boots at the two boys. Almost sheepishly the soldiers collected their property and left without further trouble.

The third night two more boys joined, and the group started singing "Onward Christian Soldiers." That night no boots came, and the boys enjoyed a happy fellowship together. Each night more boys joined until there were twenty gathering each night for a prayer band. And then when lights dimmed, Jack's side of the barracks became respectfully silent. Throughout the day whenever any of the prayer boys met, they stopped when they could to sing and pray and exchange experiences.

A few days after he arrived, Jack was called before his commanding officer. "Have you ever handled men, Zachary?"

"Yes, sir," said Jack, "I was on the trimming gang, the youngest foreman on the Canadian Pacific Railroad, two years ago."

"How many men did you have under you?"

"Thirty-two."

"Very well, I will assign fifteen men to you to take the scaffolding off the new army hospital."

Jack and his men set to work. He hoped to have the job finished before the end of the week, but by Friday noon he knew the work would not be done before the Sabbath. Instead of eating dinner, Jack went to the battalion headquarters. After saluting the officer at the desk, he said, "Sir, I would like to get an excuse slip this afternoon."

"You're not feeling well, Private Zachary?"

"Yes, sir, I'm feeling well. But the Sabbath begins before five o'clock, and I must stop working at sundown. This is my religious conviction, sir."

"You are not a Jew?" the officer queried.

"No, sir, I am not, but I keep the Sabbath for the same reason the Jews do, because God says to keep it holy."

The officer slammed his fist down on the desk. "This is the army, Private Zachary. All days are the same here."

"I must obey God and keep the Sabbath holy," Jack persisted. "It matters not what the army says or does."

At this the officer grabbed the phone. "Zachary," he snapped, "this is an order. Go and work until the regular time to quit."

"Sir, I cannot do that."

Already the sergeant was speaking into the phone. "Dispatch two guards to headquarters at once," he barked.

Jack, silently praying, stood motionless. Two guards appeared almost immediately, and flanking him on both sides, marched him to the guardhouse. Jack sat down on the one bench in the room and then took his New Testament from his tunic pocket and began to read. "And they returned..., exhorting them to continue in the faith, and that we must through much tribulation enter into the kingdom of God."

From time to time he looked up through the barred window at the guards pacing back and forth.

Before long the same two guards who had brought him to guardhouse and the sergeant who had ordered him taken there came and marched him off to see the commander of the entire batallion. The sergeant read the charge: willful disobedience of a lawful order.

Colonel Webb, the commander, took the paper from the sergeant. After pausing a moment, he asked without looking up, "Private Zachary, what is your plea? Guilty or not guilty?"

"Sir," Jack said, "I have no feeling of guilt. I must obey God rather than men."

The colonel ordered the prisoner to be taken out of the room. But in ten minutes he ordered him back. "Private Zachary," the colonel said, "where did you get the idea that you should obey God rather than men?"

"Right here, sir," Jack said, pulling the New Testament from his pocket, opening it to the text in Acts.

Taking the little book, the colonel said, "If it weren't for Great Britain you wouldn't have the privilege even of holding this book in your hands."

"But, begging your pardon, sir, if it wasn't for God's providence, Great Britain would not even be in existence."

The colonel tapped his fingertips on the desk and stared beyond Jack. Then he ordered the prisoner be taken out again. The guards led him into the hall and ordered him to be seated.

After some time the colonel sent for Jack again. "Private Zachary," he began, "your brief army record is clean. You'd better keep it that way. In fact, I am willing to help you. But you must give me a chance. You must cooperate." He paused.

"Yes, sir?" Jack answered.

"You'd better obey your orders and perform your assigned duty today and tomorrow. But by next Friday, I will know more about the situation, and I think by then you can have your excuse from military duties."

"Thank you, sir," Jack answered, "for your consideration. But I will never disobey God, even if I have to pay with my life."

His face flushing red, Colonel Webb shouted, "Take him out! Get all his army clearance papers. Then bring him back to me." Then looking Jack in the eye, he said, "We tame lions, and we will tame you."

On the double across the parade ground through the cutting wind, Jack marched back to the barracks between the two guards to get his kit and bedroll, then to the quartermaster. Jack saluted, turned in his kit, and asked for the needed paper.

"Where are you going?" asked the quartermaster.

"I'm going to Stoney Mountain Penitentiary," Jack replied.

"For guard duty?" the quartermaster asked.

"No, sir, they will be guarding me."

"Why? What have you done?" the amazed officer asked.

"I have determined to obey God rather than an army command," Jack said, "but I am so happy to have this opportunity to witness for Him who died for me." Then he briefly went on to explain his Sabbath problem.

"Young man," the officer said, "I wish I had a faith like that. I would like to pray for you, but I never learned how."

Jack's eyes shone with unshed tears. "Sir, I will pray for you," he replied.

After receiving his clearance slip, Jack marched back to the colonel. He noticed the clock on the wall. It was almost 3:30. Sabbath would come soon. Saluting the colonel he said, "Sir, here is my clearance paper." Jack looked into the steel-gray eyes of his commanding officer. "I herewith sentence you to prison for an indefinite period until you have learned to obey army orders. The warden will be instructed to put you at hard labor every Saturday. What have you to say for yourself?"

"Gladly I accept the sentence, sir, and I am ready to serve all my life, or even to die for Him who died for sinners like you and me, but I cannot work on God's holy day."

The colonel stiffened, blinked several times, and motioned the prisoner out, but for some reason the guards had him wait again in the hall. Several minutes went by. Why the delay? He had been sentenced. Why didn't they take him? It would soon be sundown.

Then once again he was called back into the commander's office. He went in, flanked by the guards, but the colonel quietly dismissed the guards and the sergeant, and Jack stood before the colonel alone.

"Zachary," Colonel Webb commanded, "step forward."

Still puzzled, Jack stepped forward. He raised his hand in a salute. "Put your hand down," the colonel said. He handed Jack a folded green slip of paper. "Young man, your faith has saved you. You will get this as long as I am in command of this battalion."

Unfolding the green slip, Jack read, "Private Zachary is excused from all military duty from Friday, 1 p.m. to Sunday 7 a.m."

"Oh, thank you, thank you, sir. God bless you, sir." Jack beamed.

The commanding officer waved him out. "Hurry and get your bedroll and kit before they close the quartermaster's office."

Thanking him once again, Jack left on the run, just barely getting to the office in time. "Look, sir! Look what I got," he pushed the green slip into the officer's hand. "I'll need my kit and bedroll after all."

The quartermaster stared first at Jack and then at the note. "How can anyone doubt that there is a God?" he said. "Young man, I wish I had a faith like yours."

When Jack got his bedroll this time, he found he had three blankets instead of the usual two. He laid his things in place in the barracks and went looking for his friends. He found them in the main drill hail clustered around the steam radiator praying. When he appeared, a shout went up and they all began to sing, "Praise God from whom all blessings flow."

As the last notes of the song faded away Jack looked up to see the commanding officer coming into the room. He went over to meet him. Jack saluted.

"What are you doing tomorrow, Zachary?" Colonel Webb asked. "Well," Jack said, "if it is a nice day, I will take a long walk early in the morning and find a quiet place to read my Bible. I love to read of God's dealings with His people."

"Will you please come to my office and talk to me?" Colonel Webb said, lowering his head.

"Why, yes, sir. It would be a great honor and privilege."

"Make it at one o'clock," the colonel suggested.

"I'll be there, sir." Jack saluted again and the colonel strode out of the room.

The next morning Jack stayed in the empty barracks praying and meditating on what he would say to the colonel. He thought of his own meager education of five grades and his life of hard work on the old homestead, but he knew that however educated or uneducated he might be, his power would have to come from God. Christ's promise to give His witnesses words to speak came to his mind. Many times since his conversion he had known the fulfillment of that promise.

At five minutes before one, Jack arrived at the office of the colonel. The officer had dismissed his staff. Jack saluted, but the older man took him by the wrist and pulled his hand down, saying, "Remember, Zachary, you will do me a favor if you don't salute me in private."

"It is hard to do that, sir. You are the senior officer in charge of this battalion."

"You may be a much higher officer in the army of the Lord," the colonel said quietly. "Sit down. Zachary; I want to tell you a story. About twenty-five years ago when I first went to the Royal Military Academy, my mother packed my trunk, and in it she put a Bible. I looked upon it as a kind of lucky charm. I did not want to let anyone see me with it, but I always took it with me when I moved. It was part of my personal effects.

"Last night for the first time I opened it. I wanted to find where it says we should obey God and where His standard of life for the human family is found. Yes, I found the Ten Commandments and the words, 'Remember the Sabbath day to keep it holy.'"

"Thank the Lord, sir," Jack interrupted. "It took me much longer to get that far in the Word of God."

"I read on," Colonel Webb continued, "and I found where it says, 'Thou shalt not kill.' What are you going to do about that? You never mentioned that yesterday."

"No, sir, that question has not come up yet. I know I will yet face it."

"When I read those words," the colonel went on, "I promised God that if we should go to France or elsewhere, I would have you so far from the front that you would never even hear the noise of war."

"Thank you, sir; I don't expect that. I will do my duty honestly and faithfully as long as I can perform it without interfering with God's requirements."

"Zachary, how did you develop such a faith that you will put God above even your country?"

Jack began to tell his experience, the torture of soul, the longing for forgiveness, the torture of a body seeking peace, and the peace of God that came with His voice and the assurance of His Spirit.

The colonel put his hand on Jack's shoulder when he had finished. "You must come to my house and tell your story to my wife and her mother." Then he paused. "Zachary, I—I must know. How—how is a person converted? How do I accept Christ as my Saviour?" he stammered.

Quietly Jack turned the pages of his Bible as he read text after text showing the colonel the way of salvation.

"But how do I accept Christ?" Colonel Webb asked, and Jack noticed the eagerness in his voice.

"Christ says, 'Him that cometh to Me I will in no wise cast out.' That is in John 6:37. All your life He has waited for you to come and say that you want to belong to Him."

"But I have been a great sinner," the colonel faltered.

"Oh, sir, Jesus came to take away sin. See, here in 1 John 1:9 it says, 'If we confess our sins, He is faithful and just to forgive us our sins, and to cleanse us from all unrighteousness.' Are you willing to give up your sins? Then He is willing to take them away. Let us kneel now and ask God to accept you as His child."

Beside the big, polished desk they knelt together, Private Jack Zachary and the tall, dignified officer.

"Dear loving heavenly Father," Jack prayed, "please accept my brother as Your child. He wants to belong to You. Oh, Father, take his sins away and give him strength and courage to do Your will. Amen."

Then while they remained on their knees the colonel in faltering words said, "God—I——I want to be—to be Your child. Please, take my sins away."

They rose, shook hands, and parted with the understanding that Jack could visit the Webbs later that day.

Not wanting to embarrass the officer by going to his house during daylight hours, Jack waited until after supper. The Webbs received him graciously, and the colonel insisted that Jack tell his story to his wife.

Once again Jack told how great things the Lord had done for him. "So you see," he concluded, "God has called me to be His witness, and

I am determined to obey Him all my life."

"How have you been received at the barracks? Have you met persecution there?" Mrs. Webb asked. Smiling a little, Jack told of the barrage of boots during prayer on the first few nights.

The colonel got to his feet from his comfortable chair. "That is too much. They must be punished," he said.

"Oh, no, sir, please don't do anything. I needed that experience as well as they did. As the apostle said, 'In all these things we are more than conquerors through Him that loved us.' You see, sir, we are now having prayer meeting in the barracks every evening, and it is so quiet you could hear a whisper."

"Prayer meeting in the barracks!" Mrs. Webb exclaimed.

"Yes, ma'am, in the barracks." Jack smiled as he stood up. "The hour is late. I must leave now. Thank you for asking me to your home, sir."

The colonel and Mrs. Webb went with him to the door. Mrs. Webb turned to her husband and said, "Art, there must be something special you can do to make Jack more comfortable."

"Thank you," Jack said, "but I'm doing all right."

But Mrs. Webb was insistent. "Really, isn't there something the colonel could do?"

"Well, yes," said Jack, a little reluctantly, "but I shouldn't even mention it."

"What is it?"

"It is concerning food. I don't eat meat, and at every meal there is meat and more meat."

"Come to my office tomorrow." The colonel clapped Jack on the shoulder. "We will put you on a special diet."

The next day at the office the colonel called Jack in. "I've got you all fixed up. Go to the officers' mess hall; ask for the head chef, and show him this order. You may pick up the utensils you need, and the chef will show you where the food is stored. Help yourself. You have access to the kitchen for two hours for each meal. If you have any difficulty let me know."

"Thank you, sir." Jack saluted. His eyes felt strangely moist, and he wiped the back of his hand quickly across them as he turned, clicking his heels, and went out.

"Thank You, God," he prayed silently as he hurried to the mess hall where he handed the colonel's orders to the head chef.

The chef looked at the paper. "This note entitles you to privileges usually reserved only for senior army officers." Then he waved toward the kitchen. "Help yourself. It's all yours."

One day Jack received a visit from a man who introduced himself as Pastor Skinner, a minister of the church that published Bible Readings. "It is the Seventh-day Adventist Church," Pastor Skinner explained. He went on to tell of the denominational organization and that the headquarters for the Manitoba Conference of which he was president was in Winnipeg.

Jack had never heard the name Seventh-day Adventist before. But now he learned of a church that kept the seventh day holy. Jack told Pastor Skinner of how God had intervened for him in his army life.

"Friend," Pastor Skinner gripped Jack's hand, "come and visit us at the conference office and Tract Society as soon as you can. Unfortunately there has been a ban placed on all public assemblies because of the flu epidemic in the city, and so our church services have had to be canceled for a while. But do visit our offices."

But before Jack had the opportunity to visit the conference office, flu broke out in the battalion for the first time. Many soldiers became ill, and on Wednesday evening Jack began to ache all over. By morning he had a high fever, and he was sent to the hospital. Since Jack's last name began with Z and the men were admitted alphabetically, he had to wait until the end of the line. Finally he stood alone before the admitting desk.

"Are your parents living?" a motherly, gray-haired nurse asked. "Who shall I notify of your illness? We're obliged to send a wire to the next of kin after the admission of each soldier."

"I have no parents," Jack said.

"Oh, you are an orphan, then."

"No, madam, I am not an orphan, but—" Jack had not realized how hard it would be to actually say the word. His eyes filled with tears, and he bit his lip.

"What happened?" the nurse asked.

Jack swallowed hard. He hadn't been letting himself think much about his homelessness, but now his weakness and fever together with the motherly woman's sympathy were almost too much for him. Bringing his voice under control with an effort, he blurted out, "I have been disowned by my parents."

"I understand how you feel," she said. "A year ago my husband was killed in action, and just last week I received a wire that my son is missing in action." Her voice broke, and she stopped to dry her eyes.

Encouraged by the sorrows they shared, Jack told the nurse of the circumstances surrounding his being disowned. She listened intently, her kind eyes never leaving his face.

"Please," she said, "give me your mother's name and address. I will send her a night letter of fifty words instead of the usual telegram. And now, young man, with a temperature of 103° you'd better get to bed at once."

As Jack weakly sank onto the clean hospital bed, his last remembered thought was one of gratitude to the kind nurse and to God who over rules all, and he prayed that his family might accept the Bible truth.

When at last he opened his eyes to consciousness it was twilight in the room, whether of evening or morning he didn't know. Puzzled, he looked around. He was no longer in the big ward where he had first been admitted, but in a room by himself. Presently an orderly came in. "Why, good morning," he said. "I'm glad to see you awake this morning."

"Oh, it's morning?" Jack asked, confused.

"Yes, it's Sunday morning. You don't remember, but you've been here three days. You've been a pretty sick soldier. Here, let's have your temperature."

Close on the heels of the orderly, his friend from the admitting desk came in. She held two papers in her hand, and she smiled. "I thank God you are better," she said. "Here is something you'll be interested in." And she handed him the two papers.

They proved to be letters. One was a copy of the night letter the nurse had sent Vasilenna Zachary. It closed with the words: "Your son is presently unconscious. He has made his peace with God and

Into the Blizzard

is ready to go. He loves you all and holds no grudge. Upon recovery, soldiers receive two weeks' sick leave."

The second letter had come from home asking Jack to come home as soon as he received his sick leave.

Jack lay back on his pillow whispering, "Thank You, God. Thank You, God," while tears rolled down his cheeks. Under the therapy of such news he knew he would recover quickly. And during the ensuing week he kept begging the doctors to let him go home.

At last the doctor told him he would be released on Friday. Immediately Jack sent a letter home informing the family of his arrival. And on Friday morning, after receiving his pay and two weeks' sick leave, he caught the morning local for home.

The long winter twilight was creeping over the snowy fields as the train pulled into Sandy Lake. Before actually coming into the station, the engine stopped to fill up at a water tank, and Jack, not wishing to embarrass his parents by arriving publicly in the town, jumped off the train and walked back a mile along the track to where the railroad cut across a corner of his father's farm. Some yards from the house he began to run across the snowy fields toward the familiar kitchen door.

10

Welcome Home

When Jack opened the door, he saw his mother standing by the stove stirring the *borsch* in the big pot.

She turned. "Jacob! Jacob!" she cried, running over to him and throwing her arms around him. They held each other a moment while Mother laughed and cried all at once. "You are all right now, Jacob?" And she kissed his cheek. "I am so happy God spared your life so I could see you again."

"Sure, Mother, I'm good as ever. Oh, this is the best thing that ever happened—to be able to come home." He shut the door quickly. "I won't let the neighbors see me. I'll just stay home with you all the time I'm here."

"Never mind the neighbors." Mother made a motion with her hands. "I am just glad you have come."

Then the door opened again and Alex and Father came in. "So there he is! We went to the station to meet you, and we didn't find you. We thought you'd decided not to come." Somewhere amidst the hubbub Mary had come in, and the laughing and crying started all over again. Everyone talking at once, and nobody listening, but Jack couldn't remember when he had ever been so happy in his life.

About that time Mother Zachary suggested that they sit down and eat. He Jacob could stand a good home-cooked meal, she insisted.

"What a supper!" Jack exclaimed, having drained his bowl of the last drop of *borsch* and taking extra large helpings of his mother's *pyrohy* with onions and sour cream, crusty rye bread and butter. Then for dessert a double serving of mother's special fruitcake and wild strawberry preserves.

While they ate, Jack told of the wonderful way God had worked for him in the army. Mary and Mother Zachary dried their eyes on their aprons several times. Brother Alex nodded from time to time. Jack remembered Alex always did everything quietly. Father Zachary cleared his throat when Jack had finished. "God has been with you, my son," he said.

Supper over, Jack led the family in worship, sharing with them the great and precious promises that had become his stay. From Matthew 10 he read, "Behold, I send you forth as sheep in the midst of wolves. But beware of men: for they will deliver you up to the councils....But when they deliver you up, take no thought how or what ye shall speak: for it shall be given you in that same hour what ye shall speak....And ye shall be hated of all men for My name's sake: but he that endureth to the end shall be saved."

Jack closed the Bible. "Now let us kneel down and thank God for sparing our lives and bringing us all together again."

The family knelt while Jack prayed. "Our loving heavenly Father, we do thank You for bringing us together, though Satan had separated us. You are stronger than our enemies. Your dear Son suffered much here on earth, and our lot is sometimes hard and the path thorny, but we gladly accept our duty as Your disciples. Please accept us and our thanks, for we ask these favors in the name of our dear Saviour who died to save us all. Amen."

After the prayer Mother Zachary looked at her son with shining eyes. "Jacob, where did you get such a sweet prayer? Who wrote it, and where can we get a copy?"

"Why, Mother, when we know our heavenly Father as a friend, we can just talk to Him. He is as real to me as you and Father. Prayer is talking with God."

"Talking with God?" she asked.

"Yes, Mother, talking with God. We talk to Him as to a close friend. Christ said, 'Ye are My friends.' 'Whatsoever ye shall ask the Father in my name, He will give it you.'"

"Talking with God!" Mother Zachary repeated. "What a wonderful thought!"

A knock at the door sent Mother hurrying to admit a neighbor, Mr. Dachensky and his nephew Kristolovich. Father ushered Jack and the two men into the room adjoining the kitchen. "Friends," Father said after all were seated, "Jacob is a little mixed up; so it has been planned for you to come and straighten him out. In order to have the most profitable discussion, we will use only the Word of God for our authority, and not even the catechism."

They pulled their chairs up around the table. "Before we begin," Jack's father continued, "I would like to ask a question from the first page of the Scriptures. Here, God is creating man. In verse 26 we read, 'And God said, Let Us make man in Our image, after Our likeness.' Who is God talking to here?"

"Well, that is easy," smiled Dachensky. "God is talking to Moses."

"What did you say?" Jack asked. "This was a little before Moses' birth. Adam is being created here."

Dachensky looked at his nephew, who apparently had never run into such a question before. "Why, I think," he said with some show of confidence, "that here God spoke to Satan before he fell."

"Let us turn to the gospel of John," Jack said. "The Word of God has the answers. In chapter seventeen Christ's prayer before His death shows that He was with the Father before the world was created. Father, please read verse five."

Father read from the Ukrainian Bible, "'And now, O Father, glorify Thou Me with Thine own self with the glory which I had with Thee before the world was.'"

"That seems very clear to me," Jack said. "Now, while we have the gospel of John, let's turn to chapter one and read the first fourteen verses.'"

After these were read, Jack said, "Notice how we are told here that the One who was made flesh, the Word, was God in the beginning and was Creator with the Father; therefore, in Genesis, God is talking to His Son."

The group readily agreed with this answer; so Jack proceeded to ask the next question. "How many Persons are in the Godhead?"

The nephew answered readily, "The Father, the Son, and the Holy Spirit."

"That's right, " said Jack. "Now, where does Mary the mother of God come in? How can you logically leave Mary the mother of God out of the Godhead?"

Neither visitor answered a word.

"Mary was a saint," Jack went on. "There is no question about that, or God would never have chosen her to care for His Son. He never went to the schools of the day. He had only His mother's training. There is no doubt that she was a good person, but she is not in heaven. The Bible gives no record of her resurrection. She will be resurrected and will welcome her Son when He shall come the second time to take home His waiting saints."

"Do you mean," asked Dachensky, "that only the saints will go to heaven?"

"Yes, I do," Jack said. "Satan became a sinner and he was cast out. How could God take anyone who sins into heaven? It would be like taking Satan back secondhand. Yes, people who go to heaven will have to get rid of all their sin here. These sins must be forgiven, and no one has the right to forgive sins but God.

"Salvation is through Christ alone, because Christ is the only One who paid the ransom. He alone can erase our sins. We must recognize Him, not just as a historical Christ, but as our personal Saviour. Anyone who stands between us and our Saviour is not ordained of God. Christ said, 'If any man thirst, let him come unto Me, and drink.' Anyone who prevents a person drinking direct from Christ is not of God's planning."

Jack's father had been listening intently. "I believe he's right," he said. "After all, Christ alone has eternal life. How can anybody else give what they don't have?"

"That is interesting," Dachensky said. "You will gain honor with your knowledge of the Scriptures, but you bring sorrow to your family, because you will never get back to the mother church."

"It is not a question of getting back to the church," replied Jack, "but of eternal life or death. If we want to reach heaven, we must make sure of how to get there. We cannot accept any man's ready-made instructions. Each must study and know for himself. Christ said, 'Search the Scriptures.' The priests cannot study for the people; the people must know for themselves."

"But I'm sure that somewhere the Scriptures teach that we should confess our sins to the priest," persisted the nephew. He began leafing through the Bible.

"Maybe you're thinking of Matthew 18," said Jack, "where it says, 'If thy brother shall trespass against thee, go and tell him his fault between thee and him alone.'

"Our Saviour says to confess our faults to one another, but notice the word 'alone.' That doesn't leave room for any proxy to come in. A third party spoils the whole work of true confession.

"I can forgive you for stepping on my toe, but my father can't. Only the one concerned can forgive an injury. Whenever we sin we break God's law. Since God is concerned in every sin, only God can forgive us.

"The Bible is God's love letter to humanity. No one has any right to keep it from man. The church has tried for centuries to bar it from the people so they would be dependent on the priests for their salvation, but only One can save us. Acts 4:12 reads: 'Neither is there salvation in any other: for there is none other name under heaven given among men, whereby we must be saved.'"

Father looked up, and there was a ring of authority in his voice as he spoke. "Friends, I can see plainly that God never commanded any man to take the place of His Son on earth."

With this the discussion broke up, and the visitors went home.

The next day was Sabbath, and while Father and Alex were working around the barn, Jack with Mother and Mary talked together through the afternoon.

"Only God knows your heartfelt desires and needs, Mother," Jack said as they talked. "Just talk to Him. He understands better than anyone else."

"And if I pray to God, He will save me?" Mother Zachary asked.

"Mother, God is the only One who can save you. He is the Creator. He knows us, the creatures He has made, and He knows what we need. So He gives us His law. He is the One we must obey."

"Yes," she said, "it is coming clear to me that we don't need to be afraid of men, to disobey them, but we certainly should fear to disobey

God."

"Mother, I'm so glad you understand this. Because God is the Creator, He is the only One who can give us power to obey His commandments. We can't obey the church when it contradicts God and then expect God to reward us.

"The church without God's authority made Sunday the day of rest. God says, 'The seventh day is the Sabbath of the Lord thy God: in it thou shalt not do any work.' But the church has taken God's Sabbath and made it the busiest day in the week. Who will we obey, God or man?"

Mother turned to her daughter. "What do you think, Mary?"

The girl laid her hand on the Bible, which had so recently become dear to her. "If we want to reach heaven, Mother, we must obey God and keep His commandments."

"Yes, yes," Jack said, his heart singing at her testimony. "Christ said, 'If ye love Me, keep My commandments.' It was Christ who gave the Ten Commandments."

"What did you say?" asked Mother in surprise. "Christ gave the Ten Commandments?"

"Indeed He did," Jack said. "Christ calls them His commandments."

"If Christ gave the Ten Commandments," she said, clasping her hands in her lap, "we'd better keep them, and all of them, including the Sabbath—Subota."

"You are right, Mother," Mary smiled. "We all should keep God's Ten Commandments: I will join you, and from now on we will keep Subota and not Sunday."

Jack could hardly believe his ears. He had prayed so fervently for this very moment, but he had never expected to see it so soon. He wanted to cry, laugh, and sing all at once, but he only said, "Thank the Lord. Thank the Lord. God will bless you both. He promises a special blessing to those who keep Sabbath."

When Father heard of the decision Mother and Mary had made, he said little. For the time being, Jack simply prayed and waited, continuing to study the Word of truth with the family every evening.

During the winter months Alex went around the neighborhood sawing stovewood. He suggested one Monday that Jack help him.

"A good idea," Jack agreed. "I need some outdoor exercise." Each day Jack worked hard cutting wood and spent the evenings indoors studying the Bible with the family. On Friday the boys worked at a neighbor's three miles away. After dinner, Jack walked home to get ready for Sabbath and to be on hand to encourage his mother and sister in keeping their first Sabbath.

"Jesus kept the Sabbath," Jack reminded his mother and sister. "In Luke, chapter four, we read of how 'He came to Nazareth, where He had been brought up: and, as His custom was, He went into the synagogue on the Sabbath day.' Yes, Christ respected the law. He had a habit, a custom, of keeping the Sabbath."

"What a privilege," Mother said, "to follow the example of Christ Himself!"

On Sabbath morning after breakfast Alex went to saw wood as usual, while Jack, his mother, and Mary spent the day reading the Bible and discussing God's promises.

Just as Mother and Mary had cleared away the late dinner dishes, Alex came in, and without saying a word, went straight upstairs. When he came downstairs he had on his suit and a tie.

"Mother, Jack, Mary," he said, "I will never again as long as I live work on another Sabbath."

"Thank God," breathed Jack fervently. "What made you decide, Alex?"

"Well, I worked at the Bylons' place today, and I had dinner there. You know what strict Greek Catholics the Bylons are. While we were eating, they asked me where you were, Jack. I told them you didn't work on Sabbath. They wanted to know why not, so I told them that Sabbath is a holy day. God made it at the end of creation. I also told them that God included the Sabbath in His Ten Commandments when He gave the law from Mount Sinai. When Christ came He kept it, and so did His disciples. It is still a holy day."

Jack stared at Alex. He had had no idea that his brother Alex had really been listening as he'd talked about the Sabbath with his mother and Mary.

Alex went on. "Then the old man asked me if I really believed all that I had told them. When I said, 'Yes,' he said, 'Well, why don't you keep it?' That was the last straw. I couldn't work another minute. I unhitched my horses and came home. I intend to keep the Sabbath from now on," Alex concluded.

"Thank God again," Jack exclaimed. In his short visit Mother, Mary, and Alex had been convinced of the Bible truths. If only he could get his father to take the step too before his sick leave was up.

The day came when he had to say good-bye to the home folk at Sandy Lake. Now Jack decided to spend some time visiting the Tract Society and the conference Office in Winnipeg as Pastor Skinner had suggested. He was anxious to meet other Seventh-day Adventists.

In Winnipeg at the Tract Society he met George Soper, the man who had written the letter that turned him back to studying the Sabbath. "Thank you for that letter, brother. God led you to write it," Jack told him.

Friday afternoon Pastor Skinner invited Jack home to spend the Sabbath with the family. Jack remarked about the delicious meatless meals Mrs. Skinner prepared. He also noticed that no one used tobacco, so during his stay he left his cigarettes in his coat pocket. On Sabbath Jack had his first experience of meeting with a group of like believers and hearing a sermon.

Before Jack left to go back to camp, Elder Skinner told Jack about a Christian school in Saskatchewan. "When you get out of the army, Jack, you should go to Battleford Academy and prepare yourself for the Lord's work," Elder Skinner said as Jack left for camp.

Back in camp, Jack quickly settled into army routine. Colonel Webb made Jack a special orderly whose main duties were feeding prisoners in the guardhouse, carrying messages, and taking care of the mail. In every way possible the colonel helped him, but over and over again he said, "Zachary, the army is no place for you."

Shortly after Jack's return to camp a buddy asked him if he had read the bulletin board that day.

Jack shook his head. "Why?" he asked.

"Better go read it," the young soldier winked at him. Jack hurried to the board. There he saw his name. He had received an honorable discharge. The document had been signed by the Canadian Minister of the Militia, Sydney Chilton Mewburn.

Jack ran all the way to tell Colonel Webb. Ignoring the protesting sergeant, Jack burst into the commanding officer's office.

"Did you know, sir, that I am discharged from the army? Now I can go and be a free witness for God. Thank the Lord!"

"Well," the commander smiled. "The letter worked. You remember before you went on sick leave I made you write the experience of your conversion? Well, I sent it to the war office. Sydney Mewburn is a relative of mine.

"Now don't forget to get your medical clearance, and don't leave without your pay," Colonel Webb added in a practical tone. "And don't forget to come over to the house before you take off. Mrs. Webb wants to hear all about your trip home to the family."

Jack nodded. "I will, sir, and thank you again for your kindness and help."

That evening Jack kept his promise and went to the Webb home. He told them of his being accepted back into the family again and of his mother, sister, and brother joining him in his faith.

"And now what will you do?" Mrs. Webb asked.

"I will go to a place like the school of the prophets to prepare me to witness even better," Jack said. "I have been told of such a school, It is in Battleford, Saskatchewan. I plan to go there immediately."

11

Opening Doors

As soon as Jack's papers were in order, he left the army and bought a train ticket for Battleford, Saskatchewan. As he sat in the coach, watching the bleak wintry fields pass the windows of the train, he wondered about Battleford Academy and what he was doing. Would the academy be the place where he could learn better how to witness for his heavenly Father? He reached into his pocket and pulled out a cigarette, and lit it.

As Jack puffed on the cigarette, a small boy skipped down the aisle and stopped to watch Jack blowing rings of smoke. Jack felt strangely uncomfortable as the little fellow stared at him. He took the cigarette and ground it out under his heel.

"Hello!" He smiled at the boy. "Where are you going?"

"I'm going to Battleford Academy to visit relatives."

Jack sat up straight in his seat. "You mean the Seventh-day Adventist school at Battleford?"

"Yes," the boy answered. "My daddy is on the school board."

"Well!" Jack exclaimed. "I'm going there too. Is your father on the train?"

"No, but my mother is. Just a minute. I'll go get her." And the boy turned and darted through the coach.

Jack reached into his pocket for another cigarette. Then he remembered his weekend with the Skinners. No one in the family had smoked. Nor had anyone at the Tract Society. In fact, as Jack thought of it, he had never seen any of the Seventh-day Adventist people smoking. Probably there would be no smoking at the school either. Jack took out the whole package of cigarettes from his pocket and dropped them behind the seat. He determined he would never smoke again.

There was the little boy coming toward him again, holding fast to the hand of a lady Jack decided must be the mother. The lady smiled at Jack and introduced herself.

"I am Mrs. Wissner, and this is my son Ollie. My husband is the treasurer of the Saskatchewan Conference of Seventh-day Adventists. Now, Ollie tells me you are on your way to the academy." Mrs. Wissner and Ollie sat down beside Jack and told him about the school and its program.

The time passed so pleasantly and quickly after he met Mrs. Wissner and the boy that Jack was startled when the conductor came through the coach calling, "Battleford, North Battleford, next stop."

"Come along with us," Jack's new-found friend suggested. "The school sleigh is here to take us to the school. There will be room for you. Besides, it will be late when we reach the campus, and you must come to the house and have some supper. Then we'll go over to the boys' dormitory with you."

Jack thanked the lady. One thing that impressed him with all the people he had met who kept the Sabbath was their warm friendliness. They kept not only the letter of the law but the spirit of it too, Jack decided.

On the ride to the school, Jack felt right at home as Mrs. Wissner and Ollie chatted with him. Arriving at the home of the Wissners' relatives, he was welcomed as if he were one of the family.

After a tasty meal and a short visit, the man of the house said, "It is late. Lights go out in the dormitory rooms before 9:30. We'd better take you over and introduce you to the preceptor in charge of the men's dormitory."

Jack thanked his new friends and put on his coat and took his small suitcase. He and his new friend walked the short distance to the big building that housed the school. "The girls are on the second floor, boys on the third, classes and administration on the first floor, and the dining room and kitchen in the basement," the man said, ringing the doorbell.

A pleasant-looking young man opened the door. "Professor Salisbury, this is Jack Zachary. He's come to school," the man introduced Jack.

The dean of men, or "preceptor," greeted Jack kindly. "You'll have to share a double bed with another fellow," he explained, leading the way up the stairs and through the dimly lighted hall. "You've arrived late, and we have no more vacant rooms or extra furniture.

"Probably your roommate is asleep, as it's after 'lights out.' But if you crawl in quietly, I don't think you'll bother him."

Jack crept softly into the room, laid down his few belongings, and after undressing by the dim light from the hall and saying a short prayer, climbed into bed beside his sleeping roommate. Weary after his long journey, he was soon asleep.

A loud bell woke him. Where was he? Then he noticed that his roommate was already up and dressing. They introduced themselves.

"Hurry and dress, Jack. We've no time to talk just now," the roommate said as another bell rang. "That's for breakfast," he added. "Follow me."

Jack followed him along the hall, down the stairs, and into a large room in the basement where over a hundred young people sat around white-covered tables, waiting.

The preceptor stood up and read from the Bible and led the group in prayer. Now Jack felt better. He looked around at the calm, happy faces. Surely this must be one of the schools of the prophets, he thought to himself.

Some of the girls began carrying the dishes of food to the tables, just as if this were a family meal—large bowls of steaming oatmeal, boiled eggs, platters of crusty whole wheat bread, dishes of blueberry preserves, and tall pitchers of milk. There seemed to be plenty of everything. Jack glanced over at his roommate, who was talking quietly with a pretty, brown-haired girl across the table. "Why, he's probably a farm boy like me," Jack decided, reaching for another slice of bread to eat with his blueberries.

Breakfast over, Jack went to register for classes. There were no placement tests in those days, and Jack could remember only that the last time he had been in school he had been in the fifth grade. More than anything, he wanted to study the Bible. But some of the teachers suggested he be placed in the elementary school in the fifth grade with ten-year-olds. Before the day passed Jack felt bored and several times the students taunted him, but he determined to finish the school year.

Jack enjoyed the hard work on the school farm, snowball fights, wrestling in the snow with the other fellows; but above all, he loved the quiet of the worship hour morning and evening, God's closeness as the Sabbath peace stole over the campus on Friday evening at vespers, and the glad courage that came to him while worshiping with his fellow students on the Sabbath day.

He wrote to John and Annie back in Moline, and told them of his desire to be baptized now that he had found the true church. And when school ended in June, he returned home full of plans for attending the coming camp meeting and being baptized. He hoped that all his family would attend, but with so much work to be done on the farms in summer, the family felt that only Jack and his younger sister Mary could be spared.

They took the train to Winnipeg and got a ride to the campground on the Assiniboine River. Jack and Mary walked through the park to the large main tent. It was evening, and in the gathering twilight they could see dimly under the trees the rows of smaller tents where the people camped. Lights shone in the main tent. There seemed to be hundreds of people there already, and they were all singing. Jack and Mary smiled at each other. Were all these worshipers believers with them? They found seats inside just as the song leader announced the song, "The Golden Morning," and as the many voices joined in the glad chorus, Jack felt sure the angels had come to join them.

> *"O, we see the gleams of the golden morning*
> *Piercing through this night of gloom!*
>
> *O, we see the gleams of the golden morning*
> *That will burst the tomb."*

Professor W. W. Prescott got up to speak. Jack followed intently his every word, taking notes in his little notebook. He would have been glad to listen all night, but only too soon the meeting closed.

Jack observed as he stood by his sister watching the people leaving the big tent, "They look happy, Mary, don't they? These are the people of the Bible Readings, I'm sure."

He looked around. "Look, there's a sign on that tent over there. See! 'Manitoba Tract Society.'" He led Mary through the crowd and over to the tent. Before long he had purchased Early Writings, Steps to Christ, The Desire of Ages, and The Great Controversy. Then he found three Ukrainian tracts: "Is the End Near?" "The State of the Dead," and "The Second Coming of Christ," at three for six cents. Jack bought six sets.

"You know, Jack," Mary said, "it's already nearly ten, and we don't know where we're going to sleep yet."

"I've got Adam Croft's sister's phone number here." Jack fumbled in his pocket. "Adam told me to be sure and call her when we got to Winnipeg."

They found a phone and Jack made the call.

"She says for us to come right over and stay at her house," Jack told his sister when he hung up the receiver. "And do you know," he added, "she lives only eight blocks from here. Isn't that providential?"

All that week Jack and Mary attended meetings at the campground, returning to Adam Croft's sister's home each night. They looked forward to being baptized together the last Sabbath of camp meeting.

As the day approached, Jack wondered what he would wear. There were no baptismal robes, and he had but one suit. Also, the Assiniboine, a turbid stream, had such muddy banks that to get into the water one would sink deep in the mud. Friday afternoon Jack helped some of the men lay canvas along the bank, anchoring it in the water with stones. Then a man, hearing of Jack's need for a suit to be baptized in, loaned him one for the occasion.

The great day came! And in the afternoon the congregation gathered on the riverbank singing hymns of consecration:

"I will follow thee, my Saviour;
Thou didst shed Thy blood for me;
And though all men should forsake Thee,
By Thy grace, I'll follow Thee."

Jack walked down the canvas-covered bank into the muddy water. As he arose from the watery grave, he seemed to hear again the clear call: "Rise! Be My witness."

The next day Jack took Mary home to Sandy Lake and then returned to Winnipeg. He wanted to tell all the Ukrainian people in and around Winnipeg the good news of salvation. He decided to get all the literature he could for his people. At the Tract Society he learned that five hundred sets of the three tracts he had already purchased at camp meeting were all the material available in the Ukrainian language.

"Brother Soper," Jack said, "give me one hundred sets. I will sell all I can, and give away to those who cannot afford to buy."

"All right," the bookman smiled. "Go ahead. You won't make much, but God bless you."

Jack took a streetcar to the section of town where many of the Ukrainian people lived. He knocked on the door of one of the homes. The lady seemed pleased to meet a Christian worker who could speak her language.

"We are living in the last days of this world," Jack told her. "This little tract shows from the Bible that the end is near, and this one tells of our hope, which is the second coming of our Saviour. Such events as riots, strikes, and wars are all signs of the end."

The lady bought three sets of the tracts for twenty-five cents.

"My people are waiting for this message," Jack mused.

All afternoon he went from house to house with the tracts. And by the end of the day he had only eleven sets left. He had sold eighty-five and given away four.

Back at the Tract Society the next day, Jack asked for more Ukrainian literature. Then he added, "What about the many German and Jewish families I had to pass by because I had no literature for them, Mr. Soper?"

"We can help you out with literature for the Jewish people," Mr. Soper told him, "but not for the German," he added, shaking his head. "During the war all German literature was banned, and the ban hasn't been lifted yet."

"But they too must have literature," Jack insisted. "Let me see what I can do. I'll go to some men in government."

"Young man," Mr. Soper said, "you can't just—"

But Jack was on his way. When he returned to the office, his face beamed. "We will have German literature again, Brother Soper. God has impressed the government men that German literature should come in freely."

Once again Jack went out with literature, glad he had something to offer every family. The first day he went back to work with the German literature, he not only sold all that he had of both German and Yiddish magazines, but he sold almost twice as many Ukrainian tracts as he had before.

"Say, brother," Mr. Soper laughingly remarked one day when Jack was in the office, "we're really grateful for the way you are cleaning off our shelves."

"Well," Jack replied, "I'm glad to do it, but I'm afraid we will soon run out of literature. Then I will have to wait. Please keep it coming. I must not stop."

In less than two weeks Jack had sold or given away all the Ukrainian tracts that the Tract Society had. But in talking to Elder Skinner, the conference president, he learned that they had been working on the problem of the translation of Ukrainian literature and had contacted Dr. Perch, a linguist, from Prague University and the editor of the Presbyterian Ukrainian weekly, *Canadian Morning*. The books by Carlyle B. Haynes, Hope of the World and *The Ministry of Angels*, Elder Skinner told Jack, would soon be translated and printed in Brookfield, Illinois.

Jack decided to return to Battleford Academy in the fall along with his sister Mary, since the books were not yet ready. This time, instead of attending the elementary school, he took some academy courses, particularly Bible, his favorite subject. But early in the winter he received a letter telling how his brother Alex had broken his leg. Since there was no one left at home to help the parents, who were now up in years, Jack left school to keep the folks on the homestead.

Though Jack and Mary were the only ones of the family baptized, Mother and Alex had been keeping the Sabbath for over two years and only awaited an opportunity for baptism. John and Annie had decided to be baptized too, after Jack's many letters to them. Now on the homestead again, Jack tried to persuade his father, who still held back because he felt he couldn't give up smoking.

As the Zachary family increasingly followed the Adventist way of life in eating, drinking, working, and in recreation, they found themselves more and more cut off from community life in Sandy Lake. With a prayer for guidance they began looking for a new home for the old folks and Alex, as well as for John and Annie. Fortunately they found suitable farms in the Protestant community of Erickson a few miles away. Here in Erickson, Mother, Alex, John, Annie, and Bill Clym, a cousin, were baptized, and the little company in Erickson was organized, one of the first Ukrainian Seventh-day Adventist churches in Canada.

Jack's father's health began to fail not long after the move to Erickson. He complained of a general weakness. Jack urged him to surrender his life to God and become free from the slavery of sin. "You can quit tobacco, Dad. God will strengthen you. Trust in Him." Time after time Jack talked with his father.

"I'll do it," the old man said at last. "God is my strength." He threw away his tobacco, never to use it again. That October, with ice beginning to form on the nearby river, Helyar Zachary insisted on being baptized.

"Now, Dad, you know how a little dampness makes you worse. Wait till spring," the boys urged.

"No," the old man persisted. "I may not live till spring. God will strengthen me."

In a biting wind, the family watched the old man walk down into the frigid water of the lake. As he came up out of the water, Jack saw a radiant expression on his father's face. At last, after all those years, most of Jack Zachary's family had accepted the Bible teachings. He felt almost overcome by a deep feeling of gratitude to God. But there were still his older brother Charles and his wife and thousands of the Ukrainian people who did not know the story of salvation.

And then the word came. The first shipment of 5,000 Ukrainian *Hope of the World* had arrived from the Pacific Press branch in Brookfield, Illinois. He took the first train to Winnipeg, went to the freight sheds, and with a rented mule and buggy at fifty cents a day, loaded on the boxes of books, and set out for nearby Ukrainian settlements.

Jack went from door to door with the book *Hope of the World* in the Ukrainian language. Where he found a real interest but not enough money he would leave the book with the words, "I'll trust you. Keep the book, and I'll be back for the money next month." Some of the money he never collected. But he gave his people the opportunity to know God.

Some months later Jack went to the Tract Society in Winnipeg. Mr. Soper did not seem as happy as usual, even though Jack told him the 5,000 books were all gone. Mr. Soper pulled out the ledger and showed Jack his account. Jack looked at the bottom figure in red—$485.00. He was no accountant, but he knew he was in trouble! He would have to find a way to pay off the debt.

That winter he piled books on his toboggan and started out. The work was rugged, the weather harsh, but Jack thanked God each day for His blessings. He did well. He was more cautious in granting credit, and his sales kept up well despite the hardships he met, but he had not forgotten his debt.

In early March Jack learned that there had been a fire at the warehouse in Winnipeg where many of the books were stored, and thinking there might be some bargains, he hurried over to the Tract Society. Sure enough. There were several hundred slightly damaged books, *The Great Controversy*, which Jack got for twenty-five cents apiece. The books were in Danish, Norwegian, German, and English. Upon opening the boxes he found that only about five percent of the books were really damaged. The rest were fine once he took the wrappers off. The sales of these books got him out of the red, and he thanked God for it.

12

The Happy Epidemic

Jack had worked around and out of Winnipeg for a number of years. While he was visiting his family in Erickson one time, his mother told Jack of some distant relatives of hers, the Bespalkos, who lived in Winnipeg. "You should go and visit them, Son. They are also from the same part of the Ukraine as most of the people of Sandy Lake."

"Well," Jack said, "I'm sure they must have heard the news—well embellished too—of the Zacharys' change in religion. But I'll look them up."

Some days later he found the Bespalkos' home and dropped in to visit. Jack greeted Helen and Matthew Bespalko and their little daughter in the traditional Ukrainian fashion:

"Glory to Jesus Christ," he said.

"Forever and ever. Amen," Matthew Bespalko answered.

Helen Bespalko smiled at Jack. "You do believe in Christ our Saviour, then? You do not use the words of greeting carelessly."

"Most assuredly. There is no other name under heaven by which sinners can find pardon and be saved, only the one name of our blessed Lord Jesus Christ."

Helen's face lighted. "That is really better than I had heard about you and the family."

"Of course," Jack reminded her, taking a seat, "you had heard of us only from our former friends. We are trying to live for God and do His blessed will. We no longer take part in the things which lead us to sin, like dancing, drinking, or even smoking. We have learned from the Scriptures that our bodies are the temples of the Holy Ghost."

"Well, I guess we didn't expect this," Matthew said.

Jack went on. "We used to depend upon the priest for instruction, but this guidance was so general that it couldn't help us personally. The Scriptures, on the contrary, give us just what we need. Christ told us to read the Scriptures. The Bible is God's letter to every man. In it He tells us His plan for each of us and also for the future of the world. This present life is a period of schooling in which we learn of God and choose whether or not we will serve Him."

"But aren't we predestined to go either to heaven or hell?" Helen interrupted.

"No, indeed," replied Jack. "That would be very unreasonable. What would be fair about such an arrangement? If this is the case, why preach the gospel? Why have a church? Why give people a choice, if there is no choice?"

Noting the interest both his cousins were showing, Jack contirued: "The Bible says that God gave His only Son, and the reason given is that 'God so loved the world.' The promise is that whosoever believes on that Son will not perish but have a life of ageless ages. You see, it is we who make the choice whether we want to live or perish. We choose either life or death."

"It all seems very reasonable," Matthew said.

"How would you two like to study more of these important truths?" Jack asked. "Whenever I am in the city I will come and study with you. Get yourselves some Bibles. What do you say?"

"Oh, that would be wonderful," Helen answered. "Don't you think so, Matt?" And her husband nodded his agreement.

In two weeks Jack returned to their home and found them studying the Bible together. "I'm trying to get my brother Alex to study too," Helen told Jack, "but he isn't very interested. He reads Ukrainian, and I have a hard time finding the same texts in the Ukrainian Bible."

After that, as they studied, they looked up all the texts in both the Ukrainian and English Bibles and Helen marked them in red.

"During the weeks while I'm gone, you can show these texts to your brother," Jack suggested.

At the beginning of one of the studies Helen said, "The trouble

100

with Alex is that he doesn't believe in hellfire that torments people without end."

"Well, as a matter of fact," Jack answered, "the Holy Scriptures don't teach that either. Don't you remember in John 3:16 we read what happens to those who don't accept Christ? They will 'perish,' stop living. You can't stop living and yet be tormented consciously. Solomon said that 'the living know that they shall die: but the dead know not anything....Neither have they any more a portion forever in anything that is done under the sun.' That's in Ecclesiastes 9:5, 6."

"Well, I never heard that before," Matthew spoke up.

"Eternal life," Jack continued, "is received when we accept Christ. We join God's family as His sons and daughters and begin a new life. Jesus called it the new birth. This is the only way mankind can have immortality." They looked up verses in 1 John 5. "Mark them for Alex," Jack suggested.

They studied on and on about the state of the dead and the resurrection.

It was late when Jack left the Bespalkos that night. "Study over what we have talked about, and we'll talk about it again when I return," Jack said in parting.

"The Bible does speak of hellfire. What does it mean?" Helen asked Jack almost the first thing upon his return.

"There will be a fire, most certainly," Jack said when they were seated around the table with their Bibles. "And it will be real. It will be on this earth. We read about it in Nahum 1:5, which tells us how the earth will be burned at God's presence. One of the clearest texts describing this fire is in the first three verses of Malachi, chapter four. 'For, behold, the day cometh, that shall burn as an oven; and all the proud, yea, and all that do wickedly, shall be stubble: and the day that cometh shall burn them up, saith the Lord of hosts, that it shall leave them neither root nor branch. But unto you that fear My name shall the Sun of Righteousness arise with healing in His wings....And ye shall tread down the wicked; for they shall be ashes under the soles of your feet in the day that I shall do this, saith the Lord of hosts.'"

"Why, this is very clear," Matthew said. "The fire will burn all that is evil in this world even as God destroyed wickedness once by a flood, and when the earth is purified and new, the saved ones will walk over the places where the wicked lived. I've read about the new earth in Revelation."

"This is wonderful," Helen exclaimed. "All the wicked ones will be destroyed and forgotten instead of being tormented there, a constant reminder to the saved through all eternity. Oh, I am so glad that God is not that kind of God. Just wait till Alex hears about this," she added, carefully marking the texts in red.

"After all," added Jack, "God is being as merciful as He can. The lost have rejected Christ. They did not want His peace here. Heaven would actually be a torment to them."

It was not long after this that the Bespalkos and Alex and his wife were baptized, much to Jack's joy. But soon after their baptism, Alex took his wife to a new home in northern Alberta, and Jack lost any direct contact with them for several years. Then one Sabbath Jack stopped over in Edmonton, Alberta. Elder George Solonuik, the Ukrainian minister, had planned a baptism in the church that afternoon and asked Jack to stay and help him. As the group came in, Jack recognized Alex, Helen Bespalko's brother. The first greetings over, Alex explained how be came to be there. "Jack, these are the souls God has given me," he said, indicating the others who had come. "For several months my wife and I have been studying present truth with them, and now, at last, these ten are ready to be baptized."

Jack could hardly speak for a moment. "Why, God's truth is like an epidemic, a happy epidemic, spreading from mind to mind, like a blessed infection," he thought as he looked at Alex and the ten persons ready for baptism.

13

Springs in the Desert

Now Jack became more eager than ever to bear witness to his people. But he needed more literature in the Ukrainian language. He went to Elder Skinner, the president of the Manitoba Conference, and told him his burden.

"We must have The Great Controversy translated. Dr. Perch is ready to do the translating," he said.

Elder Skinner, sitting behind his desk jotting down something on paper, looked up at Jack. "But we'll need at least $600. Where will we get $600 in this small conference? But, brother, I'll take it to the committee."

Sometime later Jack got word that if he would raise $150 and the Ukrainian believers in Canada would raise $150, the Union Conference would give the rest.

Jack set out at once to raise his $150. It was just after the Christmas holiday season. Winter was at its bleakest. But had not the Lord through His servant commanded that the book The Great Controversy go to the people?

Going back to the conference office, Jack once more went in to see Elder Skinner. "Will you please give me an introductory letter explaining the project?" he asked.

Knowing that the Ingathering campaign had begun, and not wanting to detract from it, he could see that there was the problem of territory. Then Jack remembered how God had sent rain without clouds when he had asked for the impossible.

"Do you have any territory in the conference that you have written off as hopeless?" he asked the brethren.

They stared at him. "Yes, there is such a territory. But you'll get discouraged there. It is the Fort Rouge section of Winnipeg."

"The Lord will provide," Jack announced to the brethren. And armed with the brief introductory letter from the church officials which stated his credentials, the project, and the need, he set out to work in Fort Rouge. He soon found that those who called it "unreachable" were not exaggerating. It was a conservative, wealthy community, with imposing-looking houses. Beside each door was a kind of telephone into which the caller spoke and stated his business. It was easy for the householder or the maid to say, "Not interested, thank you," and hang up.

A biting wind swept along the street, while the windows of the gray stone houses seemed to frown down upon the shivering Jack Zachary. He trudged from door to door, always praying, but everywhere it was the same. "Not interested, thank you," came the voice through the speaker, then the inevitable click, and Jack was left staring at the heavy, closed door.

On and on he went, pulling his coat collar up as high as he could to shut out the biting wind. Five houses. Ten. Twenty. No one would let him in. His fingers became stiff and his feet numb. He decided to run back to the railway station and warm himself in the waiting room. While hovering over the steam radiator in the almost empty waiting room, Jack prayed. Then when he could feel his feet again, and his fingers had limbered up and his teeth had stopped chattering, he set out once more with determination.

On the corner stood a large, imposing house. Jack went up to the door, rang the bell and picked up the tube to speak into.

"Hello!" a woman's voice came to him. Then a pause. "This is Miss Corliss. What can I do for you?"

"Miss Corliss," Jack spoke up quickly, "I have something to tell you."

"My maid is out," Miss Corliss replied, "but go ahead."

"I would like to come inside and talk," Jack answered. "I am not much of a salesman over the phone. I am doing missionary work for the Ukrainian people, and I would like to give you a chance to help in this important work. May I come in, please?" He wondered if she would open the door for him. If she did, he felt sure it would be an answer to prayer; for he was a stranger, and Miss Corliss had admitted that her maid was out.

There was a click. The door opened. There stood a gray-haired lady in her sixties.

"Miss Corliss," Jack began, "I haven't had much success getting into the homes in this area. I do thank you so much for inviting me in. I have a letter here introducing my work." He handed the lady the letter.

"If I had my way," Miss Corliss said, after glancing at the letter, "I would take all these foreigners and ship them out of the country. Since those people came to this city, we've had more fighting, stealing, murders, and suicides. It's shocking."

"Yes, Miss Corliss, I understand how you feel. But people who do those things need our help. Christ died for them too. We must help them. This book we want to translate is what they need It will take $600 to get it translated."

Miss Corliss mumbled something and left the room. When she returned she handed Jack a check for five dollars. Jack thanked the lady and left with a singing heart, quite forgetting the twenty-five previous refusals.

At the next house he managed to get in to see Mr. Black, who Jack learned was the provincial treasurer. He looked at Jack's record.

"I'll give you three dollars," Mr. Black said, pulling three one-dollar bills from his pocket.

Feeling quite encouraged, Jack walked up to the next house, set back from the street and surrounded by spacious lawns. He rang the bell beside the massive door. There was no telephone at this entrance, he noted It was getting even colder now that darkness had set in.

A maid finally opened the door just a crack. Without waiting for Jack to speak, she said, "I am sure Mr. Chambers would not be interested."

Jack thought fast. "I have a letter for Mr. Chambers. Would you please take it to him? I'll wait."

She reached for the letter and shut the door, leaving Jack standing first on one foot and then the other in the freezing north wind. It seemed an hour before the door opened again.

"Mr. Chambers will see you," the maid said.

"Thank you. Thank you very much." Jack lifted his cap and ran his fingers through his hair. The maid led him into a pleasant, warm sitting room where sat a white-haired gentleman.

"How do you do, Mr. Zachary. I very much appreciate the good work you are doing selling Bibles," Mr. Chambers smiled.

"Why, sir, how do you know I sell Bibles?"

"Mr. Zachary, I am chairman of the British and Foreign Bible Society, Western Branch, and I get your reports each month. You sell more Bibles than our regular salesmen."

Without waiting, Jack began to tell Mr. Chambers about the plan to translate a book for the Ukrainian people. "It gives the history of Christianity, starting with the early Christian church, going down through the dark ages of persecution, through the Reformation, and down to the last days," Jack told him.

"That should indeed be an interesting book for them." Mr. Chambers nodded.

"I am raising money," Jack went on, "for its translation."

Mr. Chambers put his hand to his pocket. But Jack was thinking fast. If he gives me just what he has in his pocket, I'll maybe get five dollars. At his office he might give more. "You don't need to give your donation tonight, Mr. Chambers," Jack spoke up. "I can pick it up later. I'm so glad to have this privilege to meet you." Jack pulled out his pen and record card. "Since I have a goal to reach each day, I would like to know what I may expect from you later."

"Oh," smiled Mr. Chambers, "put me down for a hundred dollars."

Jack tried to be calm as he wrote the amount down. "When shall I call on you?" he asked.

"Tomorrow morning will be fine, I'll be at the Pauline Chambers Confectionary on Ross Street, young man."

Jack thanked Mr. Chambers and left. Surely the Lord had been with him. The next morning Jack went to the large factory building on Ross Street. He told the secretary at the information desk of his appointment. The secretary phoned his message, and presently Mr. Chambers appeared and escorted him to his office.

When they were seated, the executive said, "I would like to see a copy of this book you're planning to translate."

Jack's heart sank. He didn't have a copy with him. "Now I'll lose Mr. Chambers's donation," he thought. But outwardly cheerful he said, "Why, I will bring you an English copy today."

"About three o'clock?" Mr. Chambers queried.

"Three o'clock it will be," Jack agreed.

And at the appointed time Jack arrived at the office with *The Great Controversy* bound in black leather and stamped in gold.

"I will take it home," Mr. Chambers said. "Come to the office at eleven o'clock tomorrow morning and I will give you the check."

Jack went back to his room and prayed earnestly throughout the evening that God would bless Mr. Chambers as he read the book.

Next morning at the office Mr. Chambers had the hundred-dollar check ready. "I shouldn't even have asked to see the book," he said, placing his hand on Jack's shoulder. "After all, you are Ukrainian yourself and know the needs. I could have given you the check the first night and saved you all this running around."

"Mr. Chambers, I didn't mind that, for it is all part of my training in the Lord's school to develop patience, endurance, and faith."

"That may be so." Mr. Chambers laughed. "But still I feel guilty about it, so please take this for yourself." And he handed Jack a twenty-dollar bill.

"Why, thank you, sir," Jack stammered, staring at the bill in his hand. He left Mr. Chambers and sent up a prayer of thanks and praise to his heavenly Father.

Some days later, just before noon, Jack was walking near the Bank of Nova Scotia when he again met Mr. Chambers. "Oh, good morning. How is the fund coming?"

"Well, to tell you the truth, not so good. I have not met another Mr. Chambers so my share is not raised. But I keep working and praying to find another one."

"Wait here. I will be only a minute," Mr. Chambers said. "I have some business to attend to."

When Mr. Chambers came out of the bank, he took Jack back to his office. "I'm really sorry I never thought of helping you more than

I did." Once at his desk, he called in a secretary. "No dictation, Mary, but bring us, unfolded, two copies of our executive letterhead."

When he had the sheets, he handed them to Jack. "Go to your office and get help in writing a letter of introduction to whom it may concern. Make it short. No more than three paragraphs, giving the reason for translating the book and brief details why this book was chosen. Bring it back for me to see and sign."

Jack went out with the stationary. He knew that Mr. Chambers was a member of many business clubs and associations. His signature would be a real help on an introductory letter.

That afternoon Jack and the conference president worked several hours drafting the letter. Then Jack took it to Mr. Chambers, who gladly signed it.

"Now, take my bit of advice. This is cold winter weather. Forget about those houses where people can say No so easily. Go to business houses only. I would advise the Grain Exchange Building. There are more than a hundred offices in its eight floors. Good luck, and God bless you."

The next morning Jack took the elevator to the top floor of the Grain Exchange Building and began working the offices systematically. At the first office he handed the letter to the receptionist, who scanned it, smiled, and said, "Just a minute, Mr. Zachary." Soon she returned. "To whom shall we make out the check?"

"To the Voice of Truth Translation Fund," Jack answered, knowing that the conference had just opened an account under that name. The receptionist handed him a check for twenty-five dollars. The next office donated fifteen dollars, and so it went. Jack worked carefully, not missing any offices, and calling back on any he found closed the first time. When he had finished the top floor at the end of the first day, he had $350. By the time he finished the whole building, he had $1800, and the Voice of Truth account was in a very healthy condition.

With these funds on hand the committee allocated money for Ukrainian Sabbath School lesson quarterlies, a songbook, an evangelistic fund, and a Ukrainian magazine called Voice of Truth.

The next year, calling on these same people with an added appeal for a Seventh-day Adventist Ukrainian church in Winnipeg, by

God's help Jack raised enough to pay cash for a church. The building purchased had been a Catholic church and had five rounded steeples topped by five crosses on its roof. With remodeling it became a representative place to worship, and it still stands today on the corner of Pritchard and MacGregor streets in the city of Winnipeg in Canada.

14

The Priest Who Dared

Of Jack's family, only his oldest brother, Charlie, and Charlie's wife Pearl were not Seventh-day Adventists. They were friendly, but regardless of the family's prayers and pleadings they couldn't see why they should change their beliefs. Jack knew that every chance he got, the village priest, the same one who had excommunicated him, visited Charlie and his wife and exhorted them to be faithful and to remember that only those ordained to the priesthood had the right to interpret the Scriptures.

Father Keluznyatsky, a much loved, kindly old man, had been in Sandy Lake for many years. How could he be wrong, Charlie and his wife reasoned with Jack when he visited them? Besides, there was the community. How could they bear to alienate themselves from all their old friends?

Now Jack felt strongly impressed to pray for two things: that God would open the way for him to visit with Father Keluznyatsky, and that God would use the priest to bring home to Charlie Zachary the full force of His truth.

But time went on, and nothing seemed to happen. Jack went on praying, knowing that prayers are quiet events, usually unknown to the world. Seeds sprouting under the ground make no noise, and leaves open silently; yet a tiny seed has the power to split a boulder or crack a mountain. Jack kept on praying, and quietly God's Spirit worked.

One morning while Jack waited for his breakfast at a lunch counter in Brandon, Manitoba, where he was canvassing, he noticed a familiar figure on the stool next to him.

"Father Keluznyatsky!" Jack exclaimed.

The priest turned a startled look on Jack. "Oh, it is you! What are you doing in the city?"

"I am very busy," Jack said. "People everywhere are seeking the light of the Holy Scriptures. It is a great honor and privilege to bring them the Scriptures in their own language."

The old priest gave him a long inscrutable look. "I wonder, can you come tonight to visit with me?" he asked.

For a moment Jack stared at the old priest. This was just what he had been praying for.

"What time will be most convenient?" he asked, trying not to show the excitement he felt.

"Seven o'clock will be fine. I am living alone." The priest gave Jack his address.

"Thank you. I will be there," Jack answered as Father Keluznyatsky got up to leave.

Jack quit work early that day to go home and study a little, and to pray that God's Spirit would be with him in his visit. "Why has he invited me? It can be nothing less than an answer to prayer. Oh, God, give me humility and power and the right words," he prayed.

At seven o'clock that evening, Jack rang the doorbell at the priest's home. The old man himself opened the door and smiled a welcome. He motioned Jack into the parlor. After inviting Jack to sit down, Father Keluznyatsky excused himself and left the room to return a few minutes later with a bottle of champagne.

"This is the best money can buy," he smiled. "This bottle is only on the table for very special guests, and you are one. Remember when you were a little boy bringing me my mail in the winter. Your cheeks were always so red. How a little glass of wine would warm you up fast. This is a cold night too." As he talked he bustled around, looking in drawers and into cupboards, evidently seeking a bottle opener.

But Jack raised a detaining hand. "Friend, please sit down. Let us visit first."

The old man sat down across the table, a faint, sad smile on his face. He shook his head. "You were one of the sheep of my pasture once."

"Yes, indeed, I was," Jack answered. "But there was a terrible drought in the pasture, not a green blade anywhere."

"I don't recollect such a drought." The old man shook his head.

"It was really dry," Jack continued. "All fresh water dried up. But today, I am feeding daily in the green pastures of the Lord, and He leads me beside springs of fresh water."

"Oh, Psalm 23," the priest murmured, his face reddening a little. He traced a pattern on the tablecloth with his forefinger. Then looking up he said, "Young man, I really felt guilty in doing what I did to you, yet I was performing my solemn duty as the pastor of the sheep entrusted to my care."

"I never held that against you," Jack replied, touched by his words. "My Saviour said, 'They have hated me. They will hate you. The servant is not greater than his Lord.' I am happy that He gave me strength to bear the trial cheerfully."

The priest looked away from Jack. "How is it that you have not given up and come back to your old friends who love you?" he asked.

Jack had his answer ready. "No one ever had greater love for me than my Saviour. He gave His life for me. I am ready and willing to pay whatever it may cost to follow Him." Jack paused.

The priest began tracing patterns on the tablecloth again.

"You say you have been performing your duty to safeguard the sheep entrusted to your care," Jack went on. "I can appreciate the burden you feel. But is your final goal to obey your superiors? What about the orders from the living God? He will judge the living and the dead. Have you studied and obeyed His orders?"

"As far as I have been taught," Father Keluznyatsky answered slowly.

"But these teachings," Jack continued, "have you ever compared them with the orders from heaven? It is God and God alone who holds the destiny of every soul."

Jack took out his Bible and turned to Matthew the twenty-eighth chapter. "Here is the last order Christ gave to His followers. 'Go ye therefore, and teach all nations, baptizing them...: teaching them to observe all things whatsoever I have commanded you.'

"Here, my friend, the Commander-in-Chief of the universe says to teach what He has commanded. Are you teaching that? After we have taught the people Christ's teachings, we are to bind the believers into His death, burial, and resurrection through baptism.

"The apostle Paul explains the meaning of baptism in Romans 6. 'Know ye not, that so many of us as were baptized into Jesus Christ were baptized into His death? Therefore we are buried with Him by baptism into death.' The baptism Paul is talking about is baptism by immersion which represents the death of the old life of sin, the rising to a new life by the power of God."

Jack noticed the priest's face had turned pale.

"Friend, if you are not teaching what Christ taught, you are teaching heresy, for the dictionary defines heresy as 'an opinion or doctrine at variance with fundamental truth.'"

With a haunted expression, the old priest listened, his lips some times moving, but never speaking audibly.

Jack continued quietly, "You said that I had joined the Jews in keeping the seventh day holy. You called Sunday a sign of true Christianity. Let us examine that claim." Jack read from the second chapter of Genesis, ending with the words, "'And God blessed the seventh day, and sanctified it: because that in it He had rested from all His work which God created and made.'

"Here is the record of how the rest day came into being. God rested and set an example for the human race to follow. Let us also note that no Jews were in existence at that time.

"When God gave Israel the Ten Commandments, He simply said, 'Remember the Sabbath day, to keep it holy.' He couldn't have said 'remember' if the day hadn't already existed as holy.

"The church has dared to teach doctrines that contradict the Scriptures. Then like the Jews of old, they persecute those who dissent from these heresies. I challenge you as a teacher of religious doctrine to show me a single incident where the disciples of Christ persecuted a heretic."

The old pastor shook his gray head sadly. "I'm afraid you are right," he said. "Yes, Christ's teaching is very plain. He said, 'Love your enemies.'"

"Yes," continued Jack, "you know the history of Catholicism

during the centuries of its supremacy. You can read about the martyrs persecuted during that time. And in God's Word, Revelation twenty, verse four, we read, 'And I saw the souls of them that were beheaded for the witness of Jesus, and for the word of God, and which had not worshiped the beast, neither his image, neither had received his mark upon their foreheads, or in their hands; and they lived and reigned with Christ a thousand years.'"

"How," asked the priest, "can you connect Catholicism with this text which speaks of a 'beast,' 'his name,' and 'his mark'?"

"The beast, of course, is a symbolic figure," Jack went on to explain, and then read about the "falling away," and "the son of perdition" in second Thessalonians, chapter two, verses two to four.

A look of bewilderment and fear seemed to pass over the pale face of the old man. "Do you mean—?" he gasped.

"What I mean is not important," Jack said. "Let us see what God's Word means. There is an important prophecy in Daniel 7:25 that describes this same power. Let us read it. 'And he shall speak great words against the Most High, and shall wear out the saints of the Most High, and think to change times and laws: and they shall be given into his hand until a time and times and the dividing of time.'

"You see, friend, here is the same power. He speaks against God, he persecutes the saints, and thinks he can change the law of God. When we compare the original Ten Commandments which God gave, with the Catholic version in the catechism, we see how the church has attempted to change God's law. She has taken out the second commandment which forbids image worship, and she has changed the fourth as we have already studied.

"When we turn to Revelation thirteen, we find that the first few verses describe the same power. Notice verses five to seven: 'And there was given unto him a mouth speaking great things and blasphemies; and power was given unto him to continue forty and two months. And he opened his mouth in blasphemy against God....And it was given unto him to make war with the saints.'

"You see, it's easy to recognize that this power described by John is the same power that the prophet Daniel and the apostle Paul described." Jack paused a moment and looked earnestly at his old friend. "I haven't gone into much detail tonight, but every word here supports the obvious conclusion. It is easy to recognize this beast power as the Catholic Church."

The priest said nothing as he gazed at Jack thoughtfully. "You know the Scriptures very well," he said at last, passing a trembling hand over his pallid brow.

Jack glanced at the clock. "Oh, my friend, I really had no intention of keeping you up so late. It is past midnight. I must be going. It was good to see you again and to have this heart-to-heart talk. May God bless His Word that we have heard, and give us strength and courage to obey Him rather than man."

The old man brought Jack's coat. "I am glad you came this evening to talk on the eternal things of God," he said. And as they walked to the door together, the priest added, "I admire you for your dedication to the Word of God and the way you were willing to give up everything for Him. God will bless you for your faithful witnessing."

"Thank you. Thank you." Jack grasped the hand of his old friend. Suddenly a daring thought came so forcibly to his mind that he could not suppress it. "Friend," he said, "I want you to do my brother Charlie and me a favor—a favor for which God will reward you. You know how much confidence my brother has in you, how he hangs on your every word—" Jack paused just an instant, then pressing the old man's hand, he said, "In the name of Jesus Christ our blessed Saviour I am asking you to tell them in church the whole truth about God and His law and how the seventh-day Sabbath is not Sunday, but Subota."

The dim light from the open doorway shone on the head of the old pastor, as tears streamed down his cheeks. "Son," he said, "that I will do, if those should be my last words on earth."

"God be praised for His goodness," Jack exclaimed. "Thank you. Thank you."

And two weeks after Jack had talked to the priest, he received a letter from Charlie stating that he and his family were keeping the Suhota and that they would always be keeping it. They told him how Father Keluznyatsky had preached one Sunday, after the mass, in Ukrainian. He had started with the creation of the weekly cycle and the sanctifying of the first Sabbath. He had gone on to the time of the giving of the Ten Commandments. "That law is God's eternal law," he had said, and he went on to show how Sunday had come in gradually as a kind of spite against the Jews because they rejected Christ. But the church in adopting Sunday was really following the example of heathen sun worshipers. He concluded, "There is no divine authority for the keeping of Sunday."

"He made it very plain," Charlie wrote. "There was a real buzz in the congregation that day, to be sure."

Soon after this, Charlie and his wife were baptized. Jack never saw his old friend, Father Keluznyatsky, again. Upon returning to Sandy Lake one day after a long canvassing trip, Jack learned that the old priest had died, but even to this day he hopes to meet him in the earth restored.

15

In Weariness and Hunger

That winter Jack bought a ten-foot birch toboggan, fastened a long manila rope to it, and loaded it with two hundred pounds of books and tracts. Then dressed in riding breeches, a heavy mackinaw, warm moccasins, leather leggins, mittens, and a fur cap, he was ready to take his books out in the coldest weather and in the deepest snow.

"I'll take my books all over the West until I wear out this toboggan," Jack promised Mr. Soper, the Tract Society man, at the conference office.

"Yes, brother, I believe you will do just that." Mr. Soper nodded and shook hands with Jack.

As usual, the winter weather was desperately cold. But despite the temperature, sometimes fifty or sixty degrees below zero, Jack worked faithfully and found many who were glad to have his books.

When his supplies were exhausted, he returned to Winnipeg where he usually stayed with the Skinner family. They praised God as he told of the marvelous providences that had come to him, and they prayed with him that God would continue to guide him to those who were hungering after righteousness. Many times over, Jack saw direct answers to those prayers.

Several times that winter when Jack came to Winnipeg, Mrs. Skinner found the shoulder of Jack's coat rubbed through by the rough manila rope on his toboggan. She patched the mackinaw and cooked special meals for him. Finally, his clothes mended, his body strengthened, his spirit warmed, Jack would load his toboggan again, take the train to the remote town that would be his next headquarters, and start out walking once more.

There was one region that Jack had long had a burden for. It was the settlement along Colonization Road northwest of Teulon, Manitoba. For the most part the people living there were refugees who had been given land after the first world war. Jack knew they were poor and probably would not be able to buy much, but they also needed to know God's last message.

He couldn't seem to forget those people; so finally, setting aside all other plans, he loaded his toboggan with a good supply of tracts, the little book *Steps to Christ*, and Bibles, as well as a few advance copies of the Ukrainian *Hope of the World*, by Carlyle B. Haynes, that had just come off the press. He boarded the train for Teulon, arriving in the late afternoon. During the night a blizzard came up with winds of fifty miles an hour; so Jack stayed in town all the next day visiting some interested friends, and waiting another night for the storm to blow over. The next morning dawned clear and very cold, but at nine-thirty he decided to start out. The deep new snow made the going hard. He and the sled sank at every step, but he plodded on. He tried to hurry, for he had seventeen miles to go if he was to reach the settlement by nightfall.

Finally in the late afternoon, as the long, last rays of the sun slanted across the snow, Jack spotted the first house. The small windows of a little log cabin in a clearing caught the sun and blazed like fire. Above the snowdrifts, dried sunflower heads and brown cornstalks rattled in the wind as he trudged up the snow-choked lane.

A thin wisp of smoke, the only sign of life, rose from the chimney, a welcome sight to the weary, hungry Jack. He paused a moment, remembering past nights in the homes of the poor where there were no beds or bedding to spare. Many times he had stretched out on a mat on the kitchen floor with only his overcoat to cover him. First his shoulders would be cold; then as he pulled up his coat, his uncovered feet would freeze. And often the food was scanty in those poor little homes. Before long it would be dark. His body ached with weariness, and he was very hungry. Ahead he saw some larger houses. He decided to leave the cabin in the clearing and find shelter in one of them, and leaning into his rope harness, he started on.

But just at that moment, with compelling clarity, the words of a hymn came to his mind:

> *"Pass me not, O gentle Saviour,*
> *Hear my humble cry;*
> *While on others Thou art calling,*
> *Do not pass me by."*

That was too much for Jack. What if the Lord had passed him by? Maybe someone here had waited a long time for the good news of the Saviour.

Jack stamped the snow off his moccasins, left the toboggan in the path, and with his guarantee pad and one *Hope of the World* in the carrying pockets under his coat, he knocked on the cabin door.

"Come in," a man's voice shouted from inside.

Jack opened the door and stepped into a sort of back porch. A man stood in the doorway leading into the kitchen. "Maria, Maria, come quickly!" he shouted. "This is the man."

"This is the man," he shouted again as he ushered Jack into the kitchen where the man's wife stood in the doorway of the other room. "This is the one I've been telling you about all day," the man went on. Then, turning to Jack, he said, "You are the man. Where is the red book, the one with white letters? Inside is a picture of Christ coming in the clouds with a sickle in His right hand."

Jack, very much mystified, took *Hope of the World* from his pocket. It was a red book with white letters.

"And where is the other small black book, all black with gold letters on it? You are selling this book, and now in this black book, I sign my name. I want that book. I mean the red book."

Jack held up his hand to stop the man. "Look," he said. "You never saw me or these books before. How can you talk this way?"

"Sit down," the man urged, "and I'll tell you. I saw you in my dream last night. In my dream I was going to town with a horse and buggy, and I came to a beautiful stand of wheat, yellow, ready for harvest. It had not been cut, and I wondered about it. Then I saw a man walking, carrying a scythe on his shoulder. He had on heavy winter

119

clothing of wool, and yellow heads of the wheat stuck to his clothes. He came walking up to me and showed me a book."

The man paused a moment, and his face lighted up with a glad smile. "You are the man," he said. "This is the book."

"Do you read?" Jack seemed impelled to ask. "No, but we have a little girl of nine, she has already attended two years in English public school and can also read Ukrainian very well."

The father called his daughter from the other room. She came in, smiling. Jack helped her to find Bible texts, which she read clearly. Then he handed her the book *Hope of the World* in Ukrainian. "She can read circles around me," thought Jack.

Jack left the book with the family. He felt sure the parents would have the little girl read to them the promises of God each day, and they would cherish the truth.

A few days before Christmas, Jack found himself in the isolated community of Cook's Creek. The people seemed to shy away from him, a stranger. "No doubt they have been warned about the heretic," Jack surmised. As darkness fell, the sky cleared, the moon shone out, and the cold increased, plummeting the temperature.

At every house where Jack called it was the same. They were not interested in anything new, certainly not books, anyway. At last he came to a large house where, from the scrape of fiddles and the shouts, as well as the extra sleighs outside, he concluded a dance was going on. Several dogs bore down on him, barking fiercely. Suddenly five or six young fellows came out of the house, each with a stick of stovewood in his hand, probably to throw at the dogs, Jack thought. He stepped up to one of the men. "I'd like to see the man of the house," he said.

"I'm the man of the house," one of the young men spoke up. "We don't want your presence around here," he went on. "You just keep going."

"All right, sir," Jack said politely. "Don't let me disturb your dance."

"Move on faster," they shouted, "or we'll give you some help."

Jack turned away. Now where could he go? He'd been plowing through the snow and storm all day and he was numb with cold, hunger and exhaustion. Every once in a while he ate a handful of snow, hoping to gain a little energy, but it only made him thirsty. He fought down a rising wave of discouragement. The night itself seemed to be saying, "You're not wanted here. Get going. You've got no right—"

In the still night his moccasined feet crunched loudly, and the squeak of his toboggan on the snow sounded indecently loud.

Far ahead the dogs at the next house began to bark. When he arrived, he saw a man in the gateway, as though blocking the entrance.

"Good evening, sir," Jack said. "Do you live here?"

"Yes, I do."

"I wonder if I could buy some food from you? I am about all in. I have used my last ounce of energy pulling this toboggan of Bibles and books."

"I wouldn't give you a piece of bread for ten dollars," the man replied.

"Sir, I don't believe I can make it much farther. Yours is the last house. This road leads to the Forest Reservation."

"You'd better keep moving. I don't want any frozen heretics at my gate."

"Sir, can I get a few matches? I don't smoke, so I don't carry any with me. If you would be so kind as to give me a few matches, I can make a fire in the woods and it will keep me alive until morning."

The man pulled a handful of matches out of his pocket. They were plainly visible in the clear moonlight. Jack began to be hopeful. "Oh, thank you, sir. Your matches will save my life tonight."

"Yes," said the man, evidently enjoying himself. "I have matches, but you will not get a single one." He put the matches back in his pocket. "Get on and keep going until you freeze."

Jack slumped down on his toboggan. Was his work to end here? Then he raised his head and looked at the deep forests, the vast reaches of snow. Lean, gray wolves, he knew, searched for food in those forests. Looking to his left, he caught a little glimmer of light. "Oh! There is a house back in there. That is good."

"Yes, there is a house there," said the man, "but don't go there tonight."

"Why?" asked Jack.

"There is a sick woman there, and she will be frightened to death

121

if a stranger should land there this time of night," the man answered. "It is almost ten-thirty."

"Has she any children?" Jack asked.

"Yes, she has two boys, one five and the other about sixteen."

Jack smiled. "Oh, that is fine. I'm sure she will not be afraid." And Jack rose, adjusting the rope on his shoulder.

"You are not going there," the man snarled with a curse. "It is my duty to protect her, and I'll keep you from going there."

Jack sent up a desperate, silent prayer for strength, that he might get to that house despite all obstacles. The man grabbed the back of the loaded toboggan and braced his feet ready for a tug-of-war. Jack leaned on the toboggan rope with all his strength, but it wouldn't budge. Perhaps it had frozen in. Such a thing was possible. He stepped back a moment, slackening the rope, then jumped forward. He felt the toboggan give, and with that, he took off as fast as he could.

Entering the lane that led to the other house, he increased his speed. His closely following antagonist was coming just as fast, but only because he was standing on the back of the toboggan. Then just before Jack reached the house the man jumped off and turned toward his own home.

Jack left the toboggan near a shed and knocked at the door. He noticed someone trying to see through the window, but through the heavy frost on the pane, he doubted that anyone could see out. Finally a woman opened the door.

"Good evening, madam," Jack said. "I am a stranger here. However, I am bringing the Holy Scriptures to the people in this neighborhood."

"Oh, come in," the woman urged. "We have the Holy Scriptures in our home, and we have been greatly blessed by its presence."

Jack took off his cap as he entered the house, and sat down. The lady of the house brought him her Ukrainian New Testament. Jack turned to John 3:16, and read it slowly and with great emphasis. "Yes, what love the Father had to give His Son for rebels like us. Let us rejoice that Christ is coming soon," Jack added. "He said so in John 14. What a privilege to be welcomed by the King of kings into His own home! And, best of all, it is free. Yes, Christ paid the full price for our redemption."

The woman and her little boy, who had come to stand beside her, listened with rapt attention. "Oh, sir," she cried, "please repeat all that you have told us to my husband when he comes. He is a musician, and he's playing for a dance, but he will come home soon."

The woman bustled around stirring up the fire, urging Jack to remove his heavy coat. "Have you had supper?"

"No, my last meal was breakfast in Beausejour, twenty miles away."

"Who brought you into the settlement in such stormy weather?" the lady asked. "I saw your toboggan of books."

"I got here on these two feet," Jack answered.

"What a distance to walk in this weather! You must be tired."

"Yes, I was," Jack smiled, "but our good conversation and your welcome have erased all that. I really feel refreshed."

"I am sorry," the woman went on; "the snow has kept us in for two weeks, and our cupboard is nearly bare."

"Oh, lady, you don't need to worry about me. God promised bread and water, and I am thankful for that."

"Well, we do have milk with the bread," she said. "It will give you more nourishment than water."

The little five-year-old boy, who had been standing near Jack ever since he had come in, spoke up. "Mamma, we have chickens, and they lay eggs. I will go and bring an egg to eat."

"Bless your heart," smiled his mother. "Chickens don't lay eggs in winter when it is so cold. It will be at least four months before there are any eggs." The lady poured milk into a pan and set it on the roaring wood stove. "Hot milk will make your stomach feel better," she said.

Jack sat in the warm kitchen watching the woman preparing food. "Mamma! Mamma!"

Jack turned at the sound of the boy's excited voice. He had on his coat, cap, and mittens, and in his extended hand was an egg. "God gave us an egg for this man," the child said. "I went out to the hen house, and there was an egg."

Jack jumped up and went over to touch it. "It's still warm," he exclaimed.

"A miracle in our humble house." Tears filled the woman's eyes. "Oh, God is good." She took the egg in her hand, and gazed at it a moment before dropping it into a kettle of boiling water.

While Jack was eating, the man and the teen-age son came in, and both the woman and the little boy began to talk at the same time about Jack's coming and the miracle.

Finally the man turned to Jack. "I am so glad that God sent you here. We have so many questions to ask you about the Bible. We are in a bad neighborhood, and we want to let our light shine before the people."

They talked long into the night. The next morning when Jack was ready to leave he gave the family a Bible for his board and room, and also left with them the book *Hope of the World*, for which they paid him later.

16

Perils in the Wilderness

Regardless of weather or personal discomforts Jack plodded on, pulling his toboggan loaded with literature especially for the Ukrainian people. When he found a home where the people welcomed his message, he forgot cold, hunger, and weariness. His promise to Mr. Soper that he would take his books all over the West until his toboggan wore out, he planned to fulfill. One day while working in the area around Lake Martin, some 200 miles north of Winnipeg, he noticed a few houses clustered on the far side of an arm of the lake. It would certainly be out of his way to visit those homes, but perhaps someone over there was longing for truth. "The ice on the lake must be solid enough to hold me and my toboggan," Jack decided. If he crossed on the ice, it wouldn't take nearly as long as going around the arm.

There was hardly any wind, but Jack knew the temperature hovered around sixty degrees below zero. He began to run. At first it was hard going, for clumps of bulrushes stuck their heads up above the drifts that had sifted around them. Farther out the ice seemed to be flat and smooth. Jack had to slow his pace because of the danger of air holes around the bulrushes and weeds. Suddenly he went down as if into a well. Struggling to the surface, he realized that he had the toboggan rope still around his waist and it was tough and long. The loaded ten-foot toboggan he hoped would make a solid anchor. Holding on to the rope, he soon pulled himself out of the freezing muddy water onto the ice where he lay panting for a moment. Then he jumped to his feet. In this weather he would freeze if he didn't keep moving.

He looped the rope over his shoulder and started to run. Already he could feel the cold creeping through his wet clothes, and he knew he was running a race with death. Quickly the icy cold began to numb his limbs. Soon all feeling was gone in his feet, then in his hands; but his mind willed his body to run, and automatically, he did for a while. He felt his knees grow stiffer at each step, and stretching his legs grew harder and harder. He kept gazing ahead at that shore, about a mile away, and the nearest cabin with a lovely plume of smoke rising from the chimney.

But soon his feet began to go out of control. His arms also felt stiff. It was hard to keep his balance. Oh, that house! Be the inhabitants friends or foes, he knew he had to reach it. But suddenly his feet, like wooden blocks, tangled with each other, and he fell. "This is the end," he thought. "I can never get up, and I will simply turn into ice and be found later." But while his brain functioned he would not give up without a struggle. With superhuman effort he tried to get to his feet, but his limbs would not obey his will. "Oh, God, help me," he prayed.

For a few minutes he lay still; then he managed to roll a little. If he could roll onto the toboggan he might still move his arms from the shoulders enough to propel himself along, he thought. Rolling slowly, he managed to flounder into position on the sled. Then, digging his wooden arms into the snow, inch by inch he propelled himself along until he reached the shore. Then he struggled again to get himself across the packed snow to that little cottage with its promise of a fire. It was late afternoon when he pushed into the yard. He pulled straight for the back door. Through the heavily frosted windows he knew no one would see him arrive. Once at the door, which opened into a shed, he rolled off the sleigh. The continual use of his arms had kept some strength in them, but the pain was excruciating. He reached the door knob and drew himself up a little, to make a thud on the kitchen door.

As the door opened, Jack half fell, and half dragged himself into the room where several children stood around staring at him.

"Please, I would like to dry myself," he gasped.

"Our parents are not at home," one of the older girls said, bringing him a chair and helping him onto it.

As the warmth thawed him, he moved his chair closer to the fire and gritted his teeth at the intense pain as the frost began to come out of his limbs. His arms were not so badly hurt, but his legs had really frozen.

Now, though in the warm house, he knew he was far from being out of danger. Even after frozen limbs should thaw, gangrene could set in. That would mean amputation, or death.

Jack worked to get his moccasins off. He had to knock off the frozen ice and mud with a piece of stovewood before they would come loose, and for the rest of the afternoon, while explaining to the children his accident, he worked at drying his clothes and rubbing the mud out of them. After his limbs had thawed completely he could not walk on his sensitive feet, and his joints were so sore he could not bear to touch them.

Late in the evening the children's parents came home. Seeing that Jack needed medical help, they decided to take him to the station where he could board a train to Winnipeg. The first train was at eight in the morning. That meant they would have to leave around four in the morning to make the twenty miles to the town of Morten before train time.

Jack gave the family a Bible and the book *Hope of the World* for all the trouble they took to help him. There was no sleeping that night for any of the adults. And long before daylight Jack, warmly bundled up, was helped into the sleigh with the father and mother. Arriving at the station just at train time, they helped him onto the train and checked his toboggan as baggage.

The train, a local, stopped often for mail, freight, and passengers. It would take all day to make the trip to Winnipeg. As the train rattled along, Jack had plenty of time to think, to thank God for his life, and to pray for guidance. If he went to one of the hospitals in Winnipeg for treatment, there would be a great deal of expense and long days of treatment.

"Dear Father," Jack prayed, "help me to know what is best to do that I may be healed quickly and return to my work."

As he prayed the thought came to him that he should go to a place where he could have the help of hydrotherapy. This thought came to him over and over. He remembered the location of several steam baths, sometimes called Turkish, Swedish, Finnish, or Russian baths.

He remembered a Russian bath on Selkirk Avenue. When the train pulled into the station, Jack managed to get off with the aid of the brakeman, who helped him to a bench in the waiting room. Leaving his toboggan checked at the station, Jack asked a redcap to help him get on a Selkirk Avenue streetcar. He told the conductor of his problem and prevailed upon him to stop the car directly in front of the bath and to help him across the street to where he could hang on to the doorknob.

But to Jack's dismay the door of the bath was locked. Probably they are closed for supper. It is about that time, he thought. Again he pounded on the door. The door opened a crack and a man said, "We are closed until seven-thirty."

"Oh, please," Jack begged. "I have had an accident, and I need help right now."

"Man, we are cleaning up, and we can't take anybody until seven-thirty," the man inside stated.

"Sir, I am not able to walk, and it will be impossible for me to wait here for two hours. In fact, it will do my limbs severe damage," Jack pleaded.

"We don't take invalids," the man said, opening the door a little wider so he could see Jack.

"Dear heavenly Father," Jack breathed, "please give me back my legs, so I can walk again and carry on Your work."

"Where is your attendant?" asked the man. "You cannot come in here like this."

"Please let me in. I will pay you. I will take all the treatments you offer. I know they will help me."

The man opened the door slowly. "All right. Come in, but remember we are not responsible if you should fall and get worse."

Jack pulled himself painfully up the steps and through the door. Oh, that warm air felt so good to his aching body. "Please may I take my steam bath right now?" he asked.

"Yes, sure," the man answered. "There's lots of heat there, and you make your own steam as you desire. But be careful not to faint. There is no attendant."

Holding on to the chairs and doorknobs, Jack dragged himself to the dressing room. How his knees hurt, and his feet felt as tender as if they were covered with boils. The man helped him undress and put on a swim suit. Then he helped him to the steam chamber. "Now I will show you what to do."

In the center of the room stood a big iron coal stove, kept red hot. Packed all around the stove, except on the firebox itself, were large stones. Wooden benches, bleached white with steam, rose in tiers around the stove, like the seats in a stadium.

The man helped Jack to the lowest bench. "Now here is a sponge," he said, handing one to Jack. "And here's the hose. Let the ice water from the hose sprinkle over on the hot stones until the steam rises. If you want more heat, climb to a higher seat. If you feel faint, turn the ice water onto your face and neck. The wooden fence around the stove will keep you from falling on the hot rocks if you should faint." With that the man left Jack in the steam room.

Jack began to pour water on the sizzling stones, and as the steam arose he breathed deeply. Soon he climbed to the next bench. Sweat streamed from every pore in his body. He climbed higher and began to feel his face burn and his head whirl, but turning the ice water full in his face, he revived with a gasp. Every once in a while he drank little sips of water, for he soon felt very thirsty. He kept climbing higher, sweating harder, and dashing himself off with ice water. After a while his joints were not so stiff or so painful, and he could feel warmth and feeling rushing back into his dead feet.

When the owner stuck his head in the room to see if all was well, Jack asked, "Do you charge according to the amount of steam?"

The man laughed, "No extra charge if you boil yourself into stew."

"Thank you, sir. I will take advantage of your liberality." Jack tried to laugh.

A little later the man returned. "Our masseur is in now. Let us give you a massage."

In the masseur's room, Jack lay face down on the couch. The masseur took oak leaves that had been tied together to make a pad, and with both hands started to give Jack a rubdown. It felt as though his skin were coming off, but the masseur paid no attention to Jack's moans and groans.

"All right, now the needle spray," he said, after having worked on Jack's legs.

Jack got off the couch. Why, he could walk without limping. He followed the man to the shower room. In the room were two standing pipes with jets six inches apart that spurted water, one pipe very hot, the other ice cold. The attendant strapped Jack's hands to a bar and he was suspended off the floor, then turned very slowly one side of him under the hot spray and the other side under the cold, alternately. The stretching loosened his joints painfully while the needle spray stung and ached until he thought he would cry with pain.

"How is that?" the owner asked.

"It's great." Jack grinned.

The man smiled and gave Jack a few more turns before taking him down, allowing him to rest on a bench in the shower room where he wriggled his toes luxuriously. He had no more pain. He felt so good he wanted to get up and run. But what about his feet? They had been badly frozen. "May I please have the same thing all over again?" he asked.

"Certainly. And we will give you a liberal discount," the man told him.

Jack went through the whole treatment again. After it was over he walked out of the bath and that same evening walked eight blocks to study the Bible at the home of a Ukrainian family who were interested in present truth and who were later baptized and became members of the Ukrainian church in Winnipeg.

Back in his territory again after his ordeal, he set to work to make up for lost time. At the close of a particularly damp, overcast day, when returning to his boarding place, Jack decided to take a shortcut, a path made by the schoolchildren across a snowy field. It would save him a mile.

Darkness crept on, and the air had grown milder. However, he well knew how suddenly a blizzard can descend on the northwest prairies, reducing visibility to zero. On the main road he could keep straight, as the lines of the fences, black against the snow, could guide him. He looked at the shortcut path again, shiny, hard packed, and clearly visible even in the twilight. He decided to risk it, and started along the trail, toboggan in tow.

He had gone about a fourth of the distance when the first snowflakes hit him, large, downy and light. Then they began to fall thicker and faster. Soon, as he looked back, he couldn't see the toboggan he was pulling.

130

Faster and faster the flakes fell. Jack started to run. In a few minutes the wind had whipped itself into gale proportions, beating the flakes into icy needles that stung his face. Desperately Jack kept running, hoping to cross the section and reach the road on the other side where the fences could guide him.

"Lost in the blizzard." The dreadful thought loomed in his mind, a hovering specter. Stories he'd heard since childhood of travelers in blizzards who'd been frozen a few yards from their homes, of limp corpses discovered after spring rains, under melting snowdrifts—all these and more sped through his mind like ghosts. But he put them away and with a wrench of the will, prayed and concentrated on the scarcely visible path.

The wind blew stronger, making him stagger, while a thick curtain of stinging snow blinded him. He barely crept along now in order not to lose the path.

So far, the way had been through shrubbery. Now he emerged into an open field, but the fresh snow, blowing so intensely from a different direction, had obliterated even the feel of the path.

Jack turned this way and that, only to find great choking snowdrifts in every direction. The more he struggled to get through, the more drifts he found. Completely exhausted, he sank down to rest on his toboggan.

"I must go in a straight line. I must keep the wind on the right side of my face," he thought to himself as he got up and started again, but it seemed impossible to keep steady. "The wind must be changing direction," he said; "or am I simply going in a circle?"

Finally his feet felt a smooth, solid surface. Was it a road? No, it was a meadow where hay had been cut and left, and the snow had blown the surface clean. Remembering to keep the wind on the right side of his face, Jack started to run again. It was easier to keep straight without the big drifts.

All at once he bumped into something solid, and his toboggan came crashing into his legs, sending him sprawling. Unhurt, he got up to examine the obstacle. It was a strawstack—and frozen solid—too solid for him to dig into for shelter. As he felt over its surface, he found the heavy twine that held it together. He pulled until he had about 200 feet of string unwound. Then, tying one end of string to his toboggan, he backed up slowly, pulling the twine through his mittened hands. Perhaps if he kept reaching out in several directions, with the help of the string he would find the road.

Then, without warning, his feet hit a low stone wall and he tripped and fell—down, down, down—until his coat caught and he turned a somersault, finally landing on his feet. He didn't have to reach out to know he was in a well. Thanks to the bitter cold, if there was water in the well it had frozen over and was cushioned with two feet of snow, so he was unhurt. He breathed a prayer of thanks; then he began to feel the walls. They were lined with wood, fastened every two feet or so with iron hoops. It was a great relief to have a moment's peace in the quiet air of the strange shelter, but somehow he had to get out of there. Looking up, he estimated he had fallen about twenty-five feet. He would have to climb up on the iron hoops around the well. Bracing himself on the first hoop, he began to climb, hoop by hoop until he could grab the top of the boards around the well, but the wood broke under the strain. Jack toppled back into the well.

This time the fall stunned him. He rested a few minutes while the dizziness cleared, again thanking God that he was unhurt. After all the exertion in his heavy clothes he was warm and exhausted. It was a temptation to rest a little longer in the comfortable hole. But Jack roused himself. He dared not rest. It could lull him to a frosty death. Once more he began to climb up the wall of the well. This time when he reached the top, he carefully tested the boards and then scrambled out into the stinging wind.

What had he done with the string? Without it he had no idea in which direction lay the strawstack and the toboggan. Groping, he began cautiously to circle the well. At last he found the string and followed it back to the toboggan.

Once more, with the wind on the right side of his face, he started out, floundering through the snow. And then he found it, the road, a hundred yards from the stack.

It had been a long shortcut.

17

In Perils by Mine Own Countrymen

One wintry Sunday morning Jack knocked at the door of a Ukrainian fisherman's house. To his knock a woman called, "Come in," and he entered to find the lady of the house sitting by her kitchen table reading the latest church journal.

"Glory to Jesus Christ." Jack introduced himself in traditional Ukrainian fashion.

"For ageless ages. Amen," the lady answered.

Jack began at once to tell her about the book, *The Great Controversy*. As he talked, he glanced at the journal in her lap. His eye caught his own name. Then between snatches of his canvass he managed to gather the main ideas written about him. There was a cartoon of a man pulling a toboggan under which was written, "Archdeceiver, Jacob Zachary. Many people fall for his sweet talk and that smile of his which hides his real purpose—to deceive Ukrainian people. He is indeed the antichrist, foretold in the prophecy of our blessed Lord, which is to come in the last days. He has already come, going about as a roaring lion, 'seeking whom he may devour.'"

Jack had left his toboggan around the corner at the last house, and he wondered if the lady had seen it.

The woman held up the paper for Jack to see. "Isn't it terrible that the antichrist is here already and deceiving the people! Poor, innocent people. Have you ever met him?"

"Oh, yes, I've been pretty close to him," Jack answered with a smile.

The woman sat back amazed, her eyes round with wonder. "Oh,

truly? How close? In the same town?"

By this time Jack wanted badly to change the subject. "Oh, yes, in the same town. By the way, the paper says something about prophecy. If you really want to learn—"

"You've seen him?" she persisted. "What does he look like?"

"He looks like anybody else. It really doesn't matter, lady. Now about this prophecy—"

"You must tell me how you met him. Sir, did you at any time meet him face to face?" Her voice dropped to a confidential whisper. "Did you look into his devilish eyes?"

Jack spoke calmly. "Yes, lady, I have met him face to face, and so have you. I am Jacob Zachary."

The woman, for a moment, sat as if stunned. Then she leaped from her chair, let out several piercing shrieks, and darted into the adjoining room slamming the door.

Jack stood up. He began to put away his prospectus, but he couldn't seem to find the place in his carrier pocket. Just then the bedroom door opened, and a large, burly man appeared looking rumpled and sleepy-eyed. Jack's first impulse was to run; but just in time he caught the eye of the man, and there was a twinkle in it. Jack decided to stand his ground, book in hand.

Large though he was, the man spoke softly. "Say," he grinned, "what kind of book is this you're selling that scared the daylights out of my wife?"

Jack needed no second invitation. He sat down with the man at the table and began to tell him the wonders of *The Great Controversy*. He had talked only a few minutes when the man said, "Excuse me a minute," and disappeared into the bedroom where his wife had gone.

Returning presently, he said, "You know something? That is the very book that little fanatic of mine needs to get her straightened out. She is hypnotized with those priests. She just worships them."

Jack continued a little longer explaining the prophecies set forth in the book.

"Get me that book as soon as you can," the fisherman said. "I'll buy it."

"I have them right around the corner," Jack said. "I'll get one immediately."

Jack got the book, and the fisherman thanked him for it. He left the couple with a prayer that the book would enlighten both the man and his wife.

The danger from his prejudiced countrymen followed Jack in the summer as well as in the winter. Early in the spring as he worked in the village of Sifton near Dauphin Lake, riding a bicycle from house to house, he found a lady who kept the Sabbath but whose husband was so bitter that he would not allow another believer near the house, or any literature to reach her. Jack had determined by God's grace to find some honest soul in the area who would accept the present truth and be an encouragement to this sister.

He had been having good financial success, but he had found little spiritual interest. He started out on a Monday morning feeling somewhat downhearted. About four miles from town he came to a barred gate closing off a long lane that led to a farmhouse. Jack let down the bars and rode his bicycle up the lane into the yard. Here he noticed a binder for harvesting grain. At first he saw no one in sight, but looking again noticed a man's feet sticking out from under the machine. "Good morning, sir," began Jack. "I want to show you a great book. Everybody in the district is buying it."

Something like a growl came from under the binder. "Just wait till I get out of here," snarled the voice, "and you'll never sell another book."

Jack waited to hear no more. He had noticed beside the man a box of tools with a three-pound ball peen hammer in it. Leaping onto his bike, he started pedaling down the lane at top speed. He could see that the gate bars, though down, would be in his way, so just as he reached the gate, he veered sharply to the right to avoid them. The quick maneuver probably saved his life, for as he turned, that three-pound hammer came hurtling through the air, just missing his head.

"By the time he picks up his hammer," Jack reckoned, "I'll be out of his reach." Jack pedaled out to the main road. Glancing back he saw the man running after him, waving his clenched fists.

"You heretic," the man shouted at Jack. "You devil, I'll catch you if I have to run all day."

135

Coming to a crossroads, Jack left the main road, taking the side road that went downhill for more than half a mile. He let the bike coast swiftly down. At the foot of the hill Jack noticed a man and his wife milking cows near the road. Looking back again, he saw that his pursuer was nowhere in sight, and feeling quite safe by this time, Jack turned in and began to show the man and his wife the book *Hope of the World*.

"We'll take that book," the man told Jack.

Looking up just then Jack saw the man with the hammer coming after him in hot pursuit. "About the money," said Jack, "could you get it right away? I'm in a hurry this morning."

The lady ran to the house, soon returning with a dollar deposit, and Jack, after thanking her quickly, jumped on his bike and sped down the lane. As he reached the road, the "hammer man" was drawing uncomfortably close, but Jack flew on to the next house another half mile away. "If this fellow keeps me hopping," grinned Jack as he thought to himself, "I'll have all my books sold before noon. Thank the Lord for a push once in a while."

But it was more than a push that the Lord achieved by means of this angry man with the ball peen hammer. For later Jack learned that the man and his wife milking cows, who bought the book and gave him a one-dollar deposit, had a daughter who became very much interested in the message. She accepted the message of the Bible and the book, and became a great friend and an encouragement to the lady in that area whose husband opposed her.

One warm day after a heavy rainstorm, Jack started out canvassing much later than usual. He began to walk fast, making up for lost time. At the first house he met a man and a woman hoeing in their garden with homemade hoes fashioned from the discs of a field harrow.

Jack began to show the man *The Great Controversy*. He was intensely interested and was about to sign an order when they heard a shout from his wife at the other end of the garden.

"You are not going to get any book," the woman shouted, coming toward Jack and the husband. "And if that salesman insists, I'll chop both your heads off." She brandished her hoe and started to run toward the men.

The husband gave Jack a startled look. "We'd better run," he whispered. "She means it."

Jack took another look at the angry woman bearing down on them. Then he and the husband took off. They ran down a hill, Jack getting some distance ahead of the husband.

The little man kept gasping as he ran, "Please—don't forget—the best binding—the best binding."

At the barn Jack started to turn in, but the man behind him shouted, "Keep straight. She'll corner us in the barn." So they ran on up over another hill. Then Jack turned into a thick grove of willows, and the man followed him. The two leaned against a tree to get their breath and wipe the perspiration from their faces.

"I believe we're safe here," the husband finally said. "I want that best binding, and I am determined to read that book in spite of her."

"Well, God bless you," Jack remarked, producing his guarantee pad once more.

"Really," the man went on, "she has such good judgment that I follow her direction most of the time. But about this book, she just doesn't understand. As soon as she finds out about it, she'll read it and like it." So saying, he firmly signed the order.

"I will pray that she will," Jack said.

"But take no chances," the husband warned. "Don't deliver the book here. I have a brother in Dauphin. That's thirty miles from here. In the fall you deliver the book there, and I'll leave the money with him."

In the fall when Jack went to deliver the book, not only was the money there, but the brother wanted a book also.

The following spring Jack began working in the Selkirk area of Manitoba. He found several children eager to learn Bible verses and hear the stories of the Bible. On Sabbath afternoons, during the summer months, he went on long hikes with them, teaching them about the Creator and the things of creation. But when the days turned cold and winter set in, an interested lady invited them to meet in her home. Soon several adults came to the studies along with the children.

Throughout the winter the meetings went on. One bitter cold Saturday night after the study closed, Jack started to open the door to leave. A folded piece of paper fell from where it had been shoved between the door and the frame.

Jack picked up the paper and read, "Zachary, if you don't leave us alone, you will find yourself at the bottom of the Red River. We mean it." There was no signature.

"What is it?" the lady of the house asked.

"It's a note to me," answered Jack. "Here, you may keep it for a souvenir."

As she read it, the lady's face flushed red, then turned white. "Somebody may be planning just that," she said. "You must not cross that river tonight. Oh, please be reasonable."

"But I must go. The Biys with whom I am staying would worry. Besides, I am to have a Bible study with them. They are almost ready to accept the truth revealed. And anyway, I work for a heavenly King who always gives me a bodyguard. Why should I be afraid? Without His permission nothing can touch me, but if my work for Him is done and He wills that I lie at the bottom of the river, I am willing. I am in His hands, come life or death."

"But you don't realize. We have some very bad elements in this neighborhood. I'm sure they wouldn't hesitate at anything." The ladies pleaded with him to stay.

"I don't want to disappoint my friends, and I mustn't disappoint my guardian angel," Jack said, bidding them good-night.

Outside, the clear, cold moonlight shone down between the bare tree branches, lighting up the path through the woods to the river. Jack walked quickly in the sharp cold. Then he began to run to keep warm. He slowed down as he came near the river. There stood a dark knot of men blocking the path ahead. In the still air he distinctly heard, "There he is. Get ready."

How many times he had been close to death! But this seemed surely to be the end of his trail. "God, help me to be brave for You," he silently prayed. Then, never changing pace, he continued to walk briskly.

"I'd better have my sword in my hand," he thought to himself as he came closer to the men. "This may be my last moment, but when they find me in the river they'll have to break my frozen fingers to get my Bible out of my hands." So thinking, he reached into his overcoat

139

pocket. The men seemed to nudge each other and began to whisper together. He could see them quite plainly now. There were four of them.

As Jack approached, never slackening his pace, the first two parted to let him through. "Good evening, boys," he said pleasantly, and the last two jumped aside so suddenly that they tumbled off the path into the deep, thick snow.

Jack smiled a little to himself as he walked quickly on. So they thought he had a weapon? Well, he did, a weapon that had never lost a battle in defense of the King of kings.

Upon reaching the Biy home, Jack told young Peter Biy of his experience and of God's watchcare. Not long after this the Biy family were baptized, and Peter gave up his work on the railroad to become a colporteur. Jack had the privilege of starting the young man out. He continued in colporteur evangelism for many years, acting as publishing secretary in several conferences and finally as general manager of the Kingsway Publishing House in Oshawa, Ontario, a Seventh-day Adventist institution.

Through the years Jack had always been conscious of his need for more formal education. Now he heard of a new school in La Grange, Illinois, the Miscellaneous Language Seminary. He decided to attend. That school year found him engrossed in church history, Ukrainian grammar, English grammar, and spelling. Then during the summer vacation he went into a large Ukrainian community in Detroit to sell books. But the people seemed fearful to let him into their homes or listen to him.

One day while working in his territory, he noticed a carload of priests pass him several times. Why not? he shrugged. There was a large church in the vicinity. Early in the afternoon he came to a big corner house and knocked on the door opening directly on the street. A middle-aged woman opened the door and invited him in.

Jack stepped inside. He found himself in a long hallway with doors on each side.

"Just go in there." The lady pointed to a door at the left of the entrance; then she went on down the hall, entering a door at the end. Thinking she had gone to tend to something in the kitchen and would soon be back, Jack pulled open the door of the room, expecting to go in and wait for her.

He stepped into the room. Six men stood facing him in a semicircle. They were all priests, dressed in black suits with circular collars. All were over six feet tall and of husky build. As one man they stepped toward him. One in the center with steely gray eyes seemed to be the spokesman. "Zachary, it wasn't enough that you turned Canada upside down. Now you've come to spread your heresy here." The priest paused. "Get this straight. This is your last day, your last hour. We have a vehicle yonder that will convey your carcass to the garbage heap."

For a moment Jack could neither move nor speak. He wanted to take out his Bible, but he knew that at the slightest move from him they would be upon him. Suddenly a text slid into his consciousness like a bullet sliding into its breech. He spoke calmly and earnestly: "'I am not ashamed of the gospel of Christ: for it is the power of God unto salvation to everyone that believeth.'"

Then he added quickly: "'Fear not, little flock; for it is your Father's good pleasure to give you the kingdom.'"

The priests gaped at him.

Jack continued. "'For God so loved the world, that He gave His only-begotten Son, that whosoever believeth in Him should not perish, but have everlasting life.'

"'Let not your heart be troubled,'" he went on: "'ye believe in God, believe also in Me. In My Father's house are many mansions—'"

At this the spokesman of the group seized Jack by the shoulder. "You damnable heretic. How dare you try to persuade holy fathers to become heretics?" With this he smashed Jack against the door, which had not clicked shut. Jack, with a twist of his body, learned from much practice wrestling with his brothers as a boy, stepped aside, and the priests landed in the hallway. The spokeman struck his head on the opposite wall. Jack jumped clear and opened the front door. One of the other priests grabbed for him, and they stumbled out into the street together. But the colporteur broke loose, and, looking up, he saw a bus stopping at the corner.

With a special spurt of speed, Jack reached the bus and boarded it.

For another week he continued to canvass in Detroit with no success; so he returned to his work in Canada.

Not long after this he realized once more that "if God be for us, who can be against us?"

While pulling his toboggan loaded with books over the snow along the railroad tracks in Manitoba, he came to a deep bank cut by the Whitemouth River. The road wound down the steep bank to a steel bridge across the river.

As Jack looked down the winding road he realized that in winter he could cross the river on the ice rather than on the bridge. A happy idea struck him. Why not have a toboggan slide? The well-cleared, icy road was wide enough to let a team of horses pass him if necessary, and there was no danger of speeding motor vehicles. He had been pulling that loaded toboggan a long time, so he settled himself, set his legs on each side to steer, and was off. With such a slick surface he started gaining momentum immediately. He sped around the first curve. This beat walking any day. Ever swifter glided the toboggan, for the road had no level places. Faster and faster he flew, round the second curve, and the third. He lost count. Surely he must be nearing the river. He was fairly whizzing now, but he couldn't see the river yet. Then he saw, less than a hundred yards away, a huge crowd of people.

"Roadway! Roadway!" he shouted, desperately trying to dig his heels into the snow. But his moccasins had smooth heels, and the road was like glass. He stretched his legs out hoping to stop himself by striking the snowbanks, but all he succeeded in doing was to cut a wide swath through the crowd. People scattered like tenpins, and screams and curses punctuated the air. He zigzagged through the crowd at top speed, finally whizzing across a hole cut in the ice and missing a priest by inches before he came to a stop in a snowbank.

Jack realized he had blundered upon the annual holy water ritual. The priest, poor man, seemed badly startled.

"Talk about casting out demons," the priest shouted, shaking a finger at Jack. "Why, here is one right here."

"I am so sorry," Jack apologized. "The road was blocked, sir, and I had no other way to pass you."

"Nobody travels today," the priest scolded. "Only demons and heretics."

Jack, not wanting to start an argument, crossed the river and began striding as fast as he could up the road on the other side.

Soon teams passed him on the road as the people went to their homes. He walked on past the houses, knowing it would be futile to try to enter anywhere after the episode at the river. Would a mob come after him when night fell? He could only pray. If God still had work for him to do, he felt sure He would spare his life.

Dinner hour passed, and Jack was hungry. Perhaps he had passed the main part of the settlement and it would be safe to enter one of the homes now. He turned in at a gate.

"Keep moving," a man in the yard growled. "Don't stop if you know what's good for you, just keep on going."

So Jack went on. Finally toward evening he came to a small grocery store and went in. "You are a brave man," the proprietor said, "to ram into a crowd of over 500 people single-handed and try to drown the priest."

"So that's the story!" Jack shook his head and smiled. "Yes," the owner went on, "that's what they all say. They just can't understand how one man could have so much courage."

"It took no courage," said Jack. "I was tired and thought I would ride down hill. Gravity did the rest. If I had known about the crowd, I would have taken the bridge, even if it is bare in spots." He bought some peanuts and some raisins and sat down in a corner at the back of the store to eat them. It felt good to get warm again.

When all other customers had left the store, the proprietor came over to Jack. "I have a message for you. There was a man in the crowd today who wants to meet you. He'd like you to stay with him overnight. I've heard the people in this area talking, and there certainly will be no safety for you anywhere else. Now listen to these directions, for if you miss, this may be your last trip." He explained carefully how Jack should find the house.

Jack thanked him and left the store. It was past seven o'clock and dark already, but Jack followed the road as he had been told, turning right at the first crossroad, then left at the second crossroad. As he passed each farm, the dogs announced his coming. But he kept praying, and the comforting words sounded in his ear, "I will never leave thee, nor forsake thee."

He came at last to the second house after the last turn. Leaving his toboggan at the gate, he walked to the door and knocked. He could hear dogs barking inside.

A man opened the door a crack and peered out. "Are you the young man who is to stay here tonight?" he asked.

"Yes, I am," Jack replied.

"Good. You are welcome. Where is your sleigh?"

"I left it by the gate," Jack said.

The man urged Jack to bring it in quickly. "We will hide it," he added. Together they lifted the toboggan onto a pile of wood in the shed and covered it with sacks.

They entered the warm kitchen, where the wife greeted Jack. "You are very brave, young man, and you must be very hungry too," she said.

"Well, not too hungry. I had some peanuts and raisins at the store," Jack told her.

"Oh, that is not proper food," the lady protested. "I will give you something hot in a minute."

And she began to set food on the table. There was Jack's favorite dish, *pyrohy*, with sour cream as well as cranberry sauce, rye bread, and milk. After his long exhausting day the food tasted wonderful.

The children, he learned, had been put to bed early, and as soon as he finished eating, the man invited him into the front room. He locked the doors, drew the blinds, and blew out the oil lamp. "I must take all precaution," he said. "I'm a marked man, as it is, and if anyone should find out that I am keeping you tonight, I might as well pack up and leave the community."

A large black iron box stove in the room sent out warmth and a wavering light. The man of the house reached for his Bible on a shelf. Then he opened the draft door on the stove. "Pull up a chair, friend," he invited. "There is enough light close to the fire so we can read. I have been reading the Bible secretly. The people in the community do not read the Bible or think for themselves. They leave everything up to the priests. But I think and read for myself. There are many things

144

that I do not understand. Now, you take Daniel, those visions, those strange beasts. What do they mean?"

Jack took out his Bible and turned to Daniel 2 and then Daniel 7. "These visions cover the world's entire history," Jack began. "They are written in symbolic language so as to hide the most obvious meaning, for these messages have had to survive the rise and fall of many nations and governments who had power to suppress the Bible. The prophecies are God's secret code which He reveals to His people."

From Daniel 2 and 7 they went on to study about the beast that received the deadly wound in Revelation 13. On into the night they studied, both completely absorbed. Suddenly an alarm went off upstairs.

"The children must have been playing with the clock," the man said.

But soon they heard the noise of the fire grates being shaken in the kitchen stove. The man glanced up at the tall clock. "It can't be five-thirty in the morning!"

"We might as well do the chores," Jack said, and together they went out to the barn.

"I want that book you have," the man told him.

"I can sell you one today, and I will give you a Bible for my stay here," Jack promised. He went out to help the man with the milking.

"Come, let's have breakfast and go to bed before the children get up. We haven't told them of your coming," the head of the house suggested.

The men went to bed after they had eaten. At noon they got up and ate the dinner prepared for them. The children were at school, the woman told them. Knowing it was important to get away from the house without being seen by neighbors, Jack asked, "Do you have a hayrack?"

The farmer nodded.

Jack suggested that he lie with his toboggan in the bottom of the hayrack. Covered with horse blankets, he could be driven secretly out of the settlement.

The man agreed. Once across the river at a deserted spot, Jack alighted from the hayrack, and the two men lifted out the toboggan.

"God bless you on your way, sir," the farmer said.

"If you are obedient to God's Word, we will meet again," Jack answered; "if not here, in God's new earth." The men shook hands and parted.

18

Not Able to Resist

As Jack went about his work, he thought of ways by which he could be more successful. As he studied the Bible, he felt impressed by the way Christ broke down prejudice among the common people. He gave practical aid to those in need. Christ did good by His divine power. We can do good by our human power, thought Jack. So he bought himself a pair of coveralls and took them along with his books.

One day he came upon a group of men standing idle around a sawmill. "What's the matter?" he asked.

"Something's happened to the valve. The cylinders aren't functioning," one of the men replied.

Inquiring for the engineer, Jack asked him to open both cylinder cocks and the throttle. "I see," Jack exclaimed. "The eccentric has slipped." Putting on his coveralls, the colporteur got to work, and within two hours he had the mill in operation.

After that, he had no trouble selling his books there.

Jack stopped at a farmhouse late one afternoon, and a middle-aged woman with a tearful face answered his knock. She seemed to be in great distress. "What is the trouble, lady? May I help?"

"Three months ago I lost my husband," the woman explained. "I thought to get a new binder because my boys didn't have much experience running farm machines. It ran perfectly a couple of days, but now it just breaks the twine and won't tie the sheaves." Two teen-age boys had appeared and were standing beside her.

Jack had noticed the new binder sitting out in the wheat field. "I'll walk over and take a look. You boys bring the horses out."

"It's no use to do that," the older boy said. "We have to wait for the factory repairman."

"I will fix it," Jack promised, "as good as any repairman, and I will even show you boys how to adjust it when I'm not here."

The boys harnessed the horses while the woman walked with the colporteur out into the field, Jack talking all the while of the hope of the resurrection.

Upon examining the binder, he soon saw the adjustment that the knotter needed. This he fixed quite easily; then as soon as the horses were hitched to it he told the boys to drive it out into the wheat. Walking behind the machine, they followed the team around the field. The binder worked perfectly, missing only one sheaf because of a gopher hole. When they returned to the starting point, Jack explained to the boys what he had done so they would be able to keep the machine adjusted.

While the boys worked on with the binder, Jack started to tell their mother about his books.

"Wait a minute," said the lady, "I want to pay you." And she offered him a ten-dollar bill.

"I would never accept a dime for doing a good turn," answered Jack. "I simply want to follow my Master, who went about doing good."

"Well, how much is the book you're selling?"

"Three dollars."

"I'll take five and give some to my relatives."

"Thank you, lady. And here is a free Bible. I always give one with an order for five books." Before giving her the Bible Jack opened it and read to her the Lord's promise to come again.

"God has indeed sent you," the woman smiled. "What a blessing to have God's Word in our home!"

At another time Jack's knock on a door brought the man of the house. He invited Jack in. While he introduced himself, Jack could hear a woman sobbing in the kitchen. He hesitated, wondering whether or not to go on.

"My wife's brother has died," the man explained. "The funeral is tomorrow, but we are so late with our seeding that it will be impossible for us to take off a whole day and go to the funeral."

"That is easily solved," Jack said. "I will do the seeding for you, and you can take your wife to the funeral."

Jack stayed with the family that night, and the next morning he and the farmer hitched up the horses to the seed drill and got the seed ready. The man and his wife left for the funeral, and Jack got to work. By the time the people returned in the late afternoon, he had finished the seeding and had done some plowing on the summer fallow.

That night he found a very receptive couple for a Bible study on death and the resurrection. The study finished, they urged him to accept payment for his work, and when he refused, they bought several books as gifts. Jack realized more and more that practical missionary work can open hearts to truth as well today as it did in Jesus' time.

Jack went on from one community to another helping where he could and bringing the good news of salvation in the books to the people. Often in church journals he found warnings from the priest about the work he was doing. One paper warned that the unity of the church was being threatened by a condemned heretic who went about like a wild beast seeking whom he might deceive. His literature was poison, the article went on to say, and must be burned. Then it said the cross should be seen on the wall of every home, or a holy picture. Homes lacking such things should be avoided like the plague.

When Jack had read this article, he decided to call on the archbishop in Winnipeg, a man that Jack's family had known well. So Jack made his way to the man's residence, A polished brass plate on the door of the imposing house stated, "Most Reverend Holy Archbishop Mykita Budka."

"Those titles belong to God," Jack said to himself as he pressed the doorbell.

The housekeeper answered the door. "Do you wish to see his holiness?"

"Indeed, I want to see him," Jack replied.

"Please write your name, address, and business on this card." She handed Jack a pen and a card.

He wrote in Ukrainian and the lady took the card. Presently she returned.

"Come in; his holiness will see you in a few minutes. He is at dinner."

Jack sat in the waiting room, hat in hand, looking around for the sign of a good Catholic. But there was not a single statue, holy picture, or crucifix to be seen. Jack rose to investigate. There were large double doors ajar, opening into the next room, and, looking for holy pictures, he peeked in. There was a picture six feet high of Pope Benedict. He stepped into the room and saw the only other picture, a small representation of the crucifixion above the door.

Jack returned to the waiting room, and presently the bishop entered, holding out his hand, which Jack grasped in a handshake.

"What happened that you have come to see me?" asked the bishop. "I did not expect you, a condemned heretic, to come here. What has happened?"

"Nothing has happened to change the situation," Jack said.

"Well, in that case," the bishop turned to leave, "I have to catch a train for the west coast in an hour, so you'd better make your business known as quickly as possible."

"If you actually have to be on the train in an hour," said Jack, "I will have to come back when you return, for my call is very important. I'll come back later."

"No, indeed not," returned the bishop. "No one comes here without my knowing his purpose."

"I'm afraid," persisted Jack, "that if we give to this problem the attention it requires, you will miss your train."

"No," the bishop said, motioning his caller to be seated, "I cannot leave until you tell me your business. You have come a distance to see me, and you are not of our fold, which makes your call even more important."

Jack sat down and drew from his pocket the paper containing the text of the bishop's address. "Are you," he asked, "according to your own definition, a true follower, or are you a heretic?" And Jack looked meaningfully about the room.

The bishop jumped to his feet, his face reddening. "Come with me and see," he said, leading the way into the next room. Turning on the light, he pointed to the large glowing picture of the pope. "There it is," smiled the bishop pointing.

"This is not a holy picture," Jack objected. "He is not even dead yet. The church doesn't make people holy until they have been dead many years."

"This most holy man is always holy," stated the bishop with dignity.

"Not according to the Word of God," Jack answered. "Only God has a right to judge a man holy, and this man has not yet been judged. Who made him a saint?"

The bishop turned quickly from contemplating the pope and pointed to the picture of the crucifixion. "There is a holy picture," he said.

"Yes," said Jack, "that is a holy picture, but see the proportions of your estimation of holiness. That picture there is twenty times bigger than this one of the crucifixion, which, besides, you have in a rather obscure place."

The bishop appeared somewhat agitated. "I'll have to make that train," he said again, looking at his watch.

"All right," said Jack, "I guess I will have to come back."

"Oh, no, no," argued the bishop, leading the way back to the sitting room. "Stay. We must finish with your business tonight."

"I have more to say about your speech," said the colporteur, "but before we get into that, I want to ask one question. Where did Catholics get the idea of making images and likenesses of God when the second commandment expressly forbids it?"

"But—but—" the archbishop sputtered.

"Of course, you have taken out the second commandment. If you will get your catechism I will compare God's Holy Word with it, and you will see that the second commandment is missing. If it were included, you would not recommend holy pictures as a test of faith."

The bishop made no move to get his catechism. "If what you say is true," he said, "we would have only nine commandments, but we do have ten."

"For a long time in your history you did have only nine," Jack answered. "But then you split the tenth and made two of it. The commandment lists what we must not covet. You have divided the list; that's all. The original law written by God has one commandment to cover all coveting. It is the tenth."

The bishop made no answer, so Jack continued. "You know, I find a great awakening among the Ukrainian people for the Word of God. If you could get Bibles authorized to be read in all the Greek Catholic churches and communities, I would buy them from you as fast as you could get them."

"Why, yes," smiled the bishop. "I have such Bibles. Wait one moment."

The cleric soon returned carrying two Bibles from the British and Foreign Bible Society, translated by Drs. Kulish, Lewickoy, and Pulie. Jack noticed that these were the same version of which he had already sold thousands.

The bishop laid the books on the table and, opening one, said, "Here it is. You can sell these Bibles all you want."

"No! No! Not these Bibles!" Jack exclaimed. "They are not authorized to be read in the Greek Catholic churches."

"What is wrong with them?"

"Well, I don't know," said Jack, "but up north your priests tell the people to burn them."

For answer the bishop whipped out his pen and wrote across the flyleaf of one of the Bibles, "This Bible is authorized to be read in all Greek Catholic churches by the authority of Archbishop Mykita Budka."

"Wait a minute. It's not that easy. According to your interpretation," Jack waved the newspaper containing the bishop's speech, "that book is poison. What difference does writing on the flyleaf make? How do you dare condemn the Bible as being poison? Christ said, 'Search the Scriptures.' And Saint Paul said, 'All Scripture...is profitable for doctrine, for reproof, for correction, for instruction in righteousness.' But the church has been the tool of Satan for generations to persecute and murder all those who had courage enough to stand in defense of the Word of God. Today, under your orders, I would also be destroyed. But thanks to God's providence I am free. You have put your own authority above the Word of God."

The bishop sat as if stunned, but Jack went on, "Christ said, 'I am the light of the world,' and all those who accept that light are to let it shine in good works all around them. But what do you do? You light candles in your churches. What a mockery! What a deception! No wonder you are afraid for people to read the Word of God. Are you not afraid to call the Word of God poison? You are only a man. God is Lord and He will judge you as well as all those who have made themselves holy and reverend by their own standards. Sir, don't you fear God and His judgment to come?"

The bishop stood up, wringing his hands, his lips moving wordlessly. Finally he said quietly, "Son, God bless you. You are well-versed in His Word, and your boldness and courage to defend Him will bring you a reward, but in this world you will have tribulation."

"Sir, that is the path of all who follow Christ truly. Christ said, 'Love your enemies,' but His teachings were ignored by the church. The humble, peaceable Waldenses were murdered in cold blood, as well as thousands of others like them. Do you approve of such acts?" Without waiting for an answer he went on: "You must, for the priest who condemned me said that anyone having the courage to eliminate heretics from society would bring honor to the church and glory to God."

"I have heard," the bishop spoke slowly, changing the subject, "about your parents and the rest of your family, how your teachings have made them what Catholic teachings could not."

"Give the credit to the powerful Word of God," Jack answered.

"They have started to fashion their lives after its teachings, and the fruit is starting to come ripe and beautiful. Christ is the vine. Without Him we can do nothing."

Jack saw that it was after eleven. He had missed his train.

"Son," the bishop said, "when your teaching makes genuine Christians out of careless and weak Catholics, go and have my blessing." And so they parted.

Some time later while in Sandy Lake visiting his family, Jack went to meet the train and get the mail. He found a crowd of people gathered at the station. The train pulled in, and presently a man appeared at the coach door. Jack recognized the man, Bishop Budka. As soon as his feet touched the station platform the whole crowd knelt as one man, and Jack was left standing alone, thinking solemnly of the plain of Dura. The bishop walked among the people, blessing them and receiving their homage. Then Jack approached him, and the two shook hands cordially.

"It's nice meeting you again," the bishop smiled.

The whole community buzzed with the episode. Had not this Zachary been excommunicated? they puzzled. The bishop, of course, was a Christian leader; Jack must be some kind of rabbi and so was respected as such.

19

Angel Hands

Then came the depression. Farmers got twenty-five cents a bushel for number one wheat, the best in the world, and twenty-five cents for eight dozen eggs. They might manage to survive on the food they could raise, but they had no money for books. The people who still had a little money, Jack decided, were the railroad men. He set out along the railroad tracks to reach them.

He arranged to deliver the books sold through the post office, COD. He had special guarantee pads made with an extra sheet providing a copy of the order for the post office as a proof that the customer had actually ordered the book. Though he took many orders without deposits, he had almost 100 percent deliveries, and those first years of the depression were some of his most successful financially.

Walking along the railroads, Jack traveled from the border of Quebec to British Columbia, on the Canadian National line in the north and the Canadian Pacific line in the south. He also walked from Flin Flon, Manitoba, to Churchill on Hudson Bay, a distance of some 700 miles, a wild wilderness area populated largely by gaunt timber wolves. He traversed the lines between Peace River, Alberta, and Dawson Creek, British Columbia, and from Wetaskiwin, Alberta, to Winnipeg, traveling more than 15,000 miles.

Walking on the railroad tracks took practice, for the ties are too close for one step and too far apart for two ties to a step. It took getting used to. In winter, walking on the tracks could be dangerous because the atmospheric conditions muffled sounds. More than once Jack saw the snowplow gliding along on the tracks only in time to jump into the drifts beside the road, the snow spray completely burying him. Also he had to remember to bury his face at a time like that, for large chunks of ice came hurtling through the air.

One winter Jack resolved to walk the tracks, stopping at all the houses along the way from the Manitoba border to the Quebec border, a distance of some 1,200 miles. At Hearst, 150 miles north of Lake Superior, he stopped at the section house for lunch, knowing that in winter the roadmen would be returning there for dinner. After eating with the men, he took several orders. Then he hitched a ride with four men who were taking a handcar about five miles down the line. From there Jack walked on about a mile when, coming to a sharp curve, he noticed that a rail had slipped to the side leaving a gap of almost two inches. Jack knew such a break would wreck a train.

He examined the spot carefully. Then to his dismay he heard a freight in the distance, and Jack knew by the sound of its whistle that it must be no more than three miles away. The train had to be stopped.

Jack began sprinting along the snowy track toward the train. The sooner he could stop it the better, but he had run perhaps 300 yards when he saw the smoke from the engine, and the train came puffing around the curve ahead with a full head of steam. Frantically he stood in the track waving, but the train came steadily on. He jumped to one side and began to wave his arms in the usual brakeman's flagging motion. There was a hissing and sneezing, and the great engine groaned to a halt.

Wading out of the snowbank, Jack climbed to the top of the cars and walked back to the caboose at the end of the train. His chest ached with each breath, and when he met the conductor he was still panting so hard he could scarcely talk. "There's a broken—a broken rail—just ahead, and," he motioned down the track, "you can't make it— The spread is almost two inches— Back train—get the—get the section crew to go ahead to repair the break—two angle bars on each side—"

The conductor signaled the engineer by the air brake, and the train started moving back. Soon the section crew had fixed the track, and the train proceeded.

"Come," the conductor said, "I will take you to the roadmaster ahead and register your prompt action in flagging the train. You saved us from derailment and, no doubt, saved the lives of the crew." But when they reached the roadmaster's office, it was closed. "I will report this to the superintendent, then," the conductor insisted.

Jack gave his name but neglected to give his address. Days later, while he was passing the Capreol station, some three hundred miles from the place where he had flagged the train, a railway guard stopped him and asked him his name. Jack knew that walking the tracks was against the law. Was he about to be arrested?

"The stationmasiter's looking for a man named Zachary," the guardsaid. "He took prompt action in stopping Seaboard Freight 405 and saved the train."

"I'm Zachary," Jack replied and followed the guard into the station. "Well, at last we've found you!" The stationmaster looked up as the guard announced him. "Have you been walking the tracks all the way from Hearst?"

Jack Zachary nodded.

"Sure is funny we haven't found you before. These wires were hot for a few days with the head office in Montreal trying to get your address."

Jack gave his address, which at the time was the Book and Bible House in Toronto, Ontario, and went on his way. Some three weeks later when he got his mail, he picked up an important-looking envelope from the Canadian National Railway executive office in Montreal. It contained a check for five dollars and a letter from the president apologizing for the meager reward, limited by law, but he thanked him for his action in saving a million-dollar train and the lives of the crew members.

Though the cash reward was small, the letter proved to be worth hundreds of dollars in cash, for Jack had only to show it to get rides on any section handcar that he met. Some days he rode across a whole division, about 150 miles, and the men who took him usually ordered books as well.

Early that spring after several days of warm rain and melting snow, the Spanish River in northern Ontario threatened to go on the rampage. One day Jack, with his prospectus in its carrier over his shoulder, walked along the railroad track that followed the river through a ravine, when he heard the clack-clackity-clack of an approaching handcar. He stepped off the track to let the car pass, but instead of zipping on by, it slowed almost to a stop.

"Young man," one of the crew members shouted, "get out of this canyon. There's a forty-foot wall of water rushing this way. It will reach here in less than an hour. Hurry and get out." Swiftly the car went on its way.

Jack started to run, looking for a road leading out. When he came to a whistle sign, he knew a railroad crossing was near. Soon he came to a crossroad and a steel bridge spanning the river. Already the water was just a foot below the bridge. He started to run across the bridge, but as he reached the other side, he noticed that a little way ahead the road already was under water. He broke off a stick from a roadside bush; then, as he came to the water, he cautiously measured the depth as he went. Fortunately it was only about six inches deep, but it was moving so swiftly that the road was fast being eaten away. Now rain began to fall as he walked on up the winding road and finally out of the canyon. By the time he reached the top of the canyon wall darkness had fallen. He could make out a railroad track that crossed the road and beyond that no sign of any habitation except one light. He started toward it. As he drew nearer he made out a building with a sign, "Chinese Restaurant." But a Chinese man opened the door and brandished a long knife at Jack. "Get away. Me kill. Me kill," he threatened.

Jack backed out across the yard to the road he'd been following. Seeing that the man had closed the door and did not seem to be following him, Jack stopped long enough to peer into the darkness for some other sign of life. Finally, high in the distance on what appeared to be a hill he saw another light, and leaving the road, he made straight for it. After walking a short way, he came to a huge rock pile, the boulders sharp and irregular as though broken by blasting. Climbing laboriously over the rugged stones, he lost sight of the light as he climbed, but reckoned that it would reappear when he reached the top. Sure enough, when the stone pile seemed to level a little, he saw the light again. Cautiously he started climbing down the other side. The pile was steeper now, the stones wet and loose, and he picked his way carefully to avoid sliding or pitching forward. Finally, thinking he had surely reached the bottom, he was about to take another step forward, when all at once two firm hands gripped his shoulders. He distinctly felt two thumbs on the back of his neck and long slim fingers pressed against his chest. The hands pulled him back and pushed him down until he was sitting on the rocks.

His heart pounded. Who was holding him? He reached behind him. There was nothing.

"Who is it?" he asked. "Who are you?" he called.

There was only silence all around him. He felt among the boulders for a stone small enough to throw and tossed it just ahead of his feet. Not hearing anything, he started to rise, but thought, No, maybe I'd better throw one more stone. He groped around for another rock when he heard a faint splash somewhere far below him.

Cold prickles of fear covered his body. It seemed that his slightest breath would move the stones under him and start the whole pile avalanching down into some terrible abyss. But he couldn't sit there longer on the edge of doom. Slowly, ever so slowly, he turned over. Painfully, with excruciating care, he inched his way up the stony pyramid. Reaching the top at last, he crawled over the summit and sat down exhausted. His legs felt weak. His whole body ached. Every time he thought of that hole, he said, "Thank You. Thank You, God, for saving my life."

At first he felt too weak to go on. He thought he would stay there till daylight. Once more he peered into the darkness, but all he could see was the light of the Chinese restaurant and that other light behind him on the hill. Then in the distance he noticed lights coming out of the ground; bobbing up and down in a row, they traveled in the direction of the restaurant. "Why, those lights must be on the caps of miners changing shifts at a mine," he spoke out loud, relieved to see some sign of life. He soon joined the men as they followed the road he had been on before.

It led to a few old buildings on a hill, one of which was a dingy hotel where the miners lodged. Over the door shone a single electric bulb, the light that had beckoned earlier. Jack went in.

"How does a fellow go about getting a room here?" he asked a nearby miner.

"That's easy." A white grin spread over the miner's dusty face. "Follow me."

Jack followed down the shadowy halls while the man opened one door after another until he found an empty room. "Here's one," he said. "Sleep tight."

The room had a bed. More than that Jack didn't notice. He slept soundly until he heard the next shift of miners come in and noticed daylight at the window. By the time he made his appearance in the lobby, a clerk sat at the desk. Jack paid for his room and then walked to the small railway station.

The rain had cleared the air, and the sun shone golden on the sprinkling of new grass and the red maple buds. Despite the warm sun on his back, Jack shivered as he gazed to the left of the road at the great mountain of jagged rock that covered the side of the hill. The boulders gleamed white like bleaching bones in the sunlight. At one edge of the pile he made out the gaping mouth of a great pit, and he shuddered. Did the sun ever reach the bottom of it?

At the railway station Jack purchased a ticket to Espinola. Then he asked the ticket agent, "Could you tell me how deep that old mine shaft is over there?" He gestured in the direction of the rock pile.

The man scratched his head. "Well, it is at least 700 feet."

"Quite a hole," Jack commented, pocketing his ticket and turning to leave. Outside once more he lifted his face toward heaven and said, "Thank You, Lord."

20

"Viva" Means Life

As the years of depression lingered, Jack found it harder and harder to make deliveries. The people wanted the books, but there was no money to pay for them. Then, too, he began to feel the results of the times of exposure to freezing weather and his having fallen through the ice in the lake and having his limbs badly frostbitten. At times in the winter his legs ached so much that it was hard to get around—then he had a decided limp. But ever in his mind was the thought that he had been called to be a witness.

At last, after much thought and prayer, Jack decided to return to Erickson for a while. He could do much to strengthen the church there, and with plenty of timber in the vicinity he could start his own logging operation.

Even while engaged in the logging business Jack Zachary found opportunities to share his faith. And although not then in the colporteur work Jack read every report in the union paper. During the summer he watched the student colporteur reports. There was one girl, a Viva Smith, who seemed to be having better success than the others. Jack wondered what she was like. He'd like to write to her and congratulate her on her work and encourage her. For beginners there was always the danger of discouragement.

One day Jack sat down with pen and paper and wrote a letter to Viva Smith. He mailed it in care of the conference office.

And several days later Viva Smith picked up her mail to find an envelope addressed in an unfamiliar handwriting. In the upper lefthand corner was the name Jack Zachary.

Jack Zachary! That was the name of the fellow her friend Mary Schmidt with whom she had been canvassing had told her about. Mary had met him at camp meeting. Her face had glowed when she had talked about him.

"Why, when he talks—people just listen, that's all. He's had such wonderful experiences," Mary had said. She'd gone on to tell about how dedicated he was, and about how he'd been disowned by his family when he'd joined the church. Viva smiled as she remembered Mary adding, "Oh, you should meet Jack. He's wonderful!"

And now she held a letter in her hand from Jack Zachary. Viva tore the letter open and read the brief note written in imperfect English. He had noticed her fine record in the union paper, he stated. He went on to say that although he was not selling books at that time, his heart would always be in that work, and he added, "Courage in the Lord. God leads those who trust Him."

For a moment Viva's head swam. Why, she had not exactly prayed to be able to meet Jack Zachary since Mary's glowing reports, but it did seem that a guiding hand was making such a friendship possible. A regular correspondence began. Viva told Jack of her childhood with her pioneer English-Irish parents in a sod house on the Alberta prairie and how from her Seventh-day Adventist parents she had learned to love God and His truth above all else. Jack told her of his early days on the homestead and of his search for truth.

She wrote about her busy life on the farm, how she had not been able to go away to boarding school until she was just past twenty. And then she had gone to Canadian Junior College at Lacombe, Alberta. She told Jack how she had been persuaded to enter the canvassing work by a Peter Biy, the publishing secretary of the conference, and he had started her out in the work.

Peter Biy, the young man to whom Jack had brought the truth back in Selkirk, Manitoba, some years ago!

Letters went back and forth between the two young people all summer. She told him she would have to leave canvassing to return home where she was needed because her mother had had a bad fall. When school opened, she could not return because of lack of funds, but once again she planned to start out in the canvassing work. She had territory in the city. Everyone thought city territory would be better for her, she wrote, than the long stretches of snowy country roads. But she sold few books and became more and more disheartened. His letters were the bright spots in the week for her.

Through the months of writing, Jack had told her of his past life, his conversion, his canvassing, and his present work running his own sawmill. Through it all shone his ever-burning faith in God. And then he suggested that she consider coming to work for him in Erickson. "I need another cook for my twelve men," he explained, "and I don't have a bookkeeper."

Now there was an opportunity at last to meet Jack Zachary. His letters had come to mean a great deal to her. But she dared not trust her feelings alone. She had too much common sense for that. Because she knew that Jack Zachary's purpose in life was one with hers, she knew she could pray for guidance, and this she did. Two days after New Year's she wrote, "I will work another week at canvassing, doing my best with God's help, and if things are not better by then, I will accept your offer."

Upon receiving her message, Jack promptly mailed her a letter encouraging her to come if God would so lead. By the next week a wire came from Viva saying, "Arriving Erickson four-o'clock train Thursday."

Thursday seemed a long way off. Jack Zachary wanted to meet Viva Smith, and now that it was coming to pass, the time dragged. In the sleeping quarters of his lumber camp Thursday morning Jack awoke while it was still dark, a strange excitement tingling through him. Through the curtained door from the kitchen he could hear the clatter of dishes and the clash of the iron stove door. Soon the smell of woodsmoke and cooking oatmeal wafted in to him.

He got up quickly. He had to give his foreman his orders, do several errands up the road, and finally go to town on what might well be one of the most important errands of his life. Before going out to meet the day, he knelt beside his rough bunk to pray: "Dear Father, if it is in Your plan, this is the day that I will see her. I wonder what she will be like. Of course, You know her and she knows You, and I believe You are leading us. Oh, Father, guide me that I may do nothing

163

against Your will. May Your gracious, powerful hand be over all."

Rising from his knees, Jack hurried out to the large common room which served the camp as kitchen, dining room, and parlor. "Morning, Annie," he said to the cook girl. "Could you give me breakfast now? I've got to get an early start today." He sat down at one end of the big table. "I'll probably be a little late tonight," he added.

"Oh, that's right," Annie grinned, a mischievous look on her broad, good-natured face. "This is the day you bring home Miss What's-hername. Smith, did you say?"

Jack helped himself from the platter Annie set in front of him. "Yes, Viva Smith," he said, surprised at the deep excitement that welled in him as he said the name.

As he finished eating, some of the camp crew began coming in for breakfast. Jack called to his foreman, "See about that upper stretch of fir today, Paul. You won't finish, with the sunset so early, but you can get started. I'll be seeing Lokensgard about that team this morning, and then I'll be going to town. Got to meet the four o'clock train."

Most of the crew had gathered around the breakfast table by this time. Jack noticed their smiles and knowing winks.

"Take good care of your lady," Paul said. "We'll all be waiting to meet her."

"Don't rush me, friend. She's not my lady yet." And, smiling, Jack turned to Annie for a last check of the list of provisions to be bought.

Stepping out into the cold morning air, he looked up at the sky where the stars had begun to pale. He hitched his horse to the cutter and started out. By the time he reached town it was nearly noon, and he had a long list of provisions to buy. He hurried from store to store. With a delay here and another there, his frustrations mounted. Suddenly he looked at his watch. It was three-thirty! The train was due at four and he still had to get to the hardware store. With a push he could make it, he decided. He hoped the train was late as it usually was. He jumped into his sleigh and flicked his whip over the flanks of his little gray horse, and the sleigh lurched forward through the drab slush of the streets.

It was just four when he finished at the hardware and urged his horse quickly on to the railroad station. As he rounded the last curve

in the road, he heard a train whistle, and disappearing through the trees was the tail end of the last coach. The train had been on time.

At the station Jack leaped from the sleigh and hitched his horse to a post. He sprang up the walk and grasped the station waiting-room doorknob. When the door opened Jack saw a tall girl in a red coat standing with her hand outstretched. She had a large suitcase at her feet.

A quick glance around the station showed no one but the stationmaster, and again Jack looked at the girl. She had a friendly face warmly sprinkled with freckles, but her expression at the moment seemed a little puzzled and uncertain.

"I am sure you are Miss Smith," he said.

The girl put out her hand. "You are Mr. Zachary," she replied.

The day had been gray and dismal, but as Jack looked into her hazel eyes and saw her warm smile, he had the distinct impression that the sun had come out, He blinked. "I'm—I'm sorry I'm late," he faltered. "Usually I'm not late, but today I had so much to do, and the train, for once, came on time, and—"

"Oh, it doesn't matter now that you're here," the girl laughed.

She has a nice voice, Jack thought, and her way of laughing makes me feel—well—just makes me feel good.

"I was on my way to find a phone to call the number you gave me," the girl said. "Did you say it was your brother's phone?"

Jack picked up her suitcase and led the way to the cutter. "Yes, that's my brother Alex's phone number I gave you. He's the mail carrier here. Lives on the edge of town. My father and mother live with him. But my camp is ten miles out. I hope you don't mind a little ride, Miss Smith."

"Oh, just call me Viva," she said, climbing into the sleigh.

"I will if you call me Jack." Jack tucked the bearskin robe around her; then he got in on his side and snapped the reins over the horse's back.

A few stray snowflakes brushed their faces as they started on the long trip. But they had so much to talk about that time passed quickly. It was dark by the time they arrived at camp. The big kitchen with its long table covered in red-patterned oilcloth, the friendly old range crackling out its heat, the warm glow of the oil lamps, the delicious smell of baked beans and warm fresh bread, all seemed to say, Welcome home.

Annie, the cook, smiled as she brought supper and placed it on the table. Then the camp boys stepped up to be introduced. After supper they excused themselves and left Jack and Viva alone. They sat in two rockers near the warm stove exchanging canvassing experiences and rocking gently. Viva began telling of how the summer before, her hired horse had broken its traces and run away, upsetting her buggy.

Dividing his attention between listening and admiring the copper glints in her auburn hair, Jack concentrated so intently that he failed to notice how his rocking chair kept creeping slowly over the uneven floor toward the curtained door of one of the sleeping rooms where the doorsill dropped several inches.

Suddenly his chair tipped backwards, and Jack went heels over head through the curtain. He heard Viva gasp. When he picked himself up and looked at Viva, they both burst out laughing.

"I forgot there was a step down there," he explained, setting his rocker straight again.

"I'm glad you're not hurt," Viva laughed.

In the kitchen the next morning Viva helped Annie as though she had always been there, and Jack thought as he watched her how home for him would always be wherever she was.

Every evening when the dishes had been cleared away Viva, following the pattern of her upbringing, would gather the few hymnbooks and bring her Bible. "It's time for worship," she would say. The young voices would join in singing favorite hymns. Then Jack would take his Bible and begin to read, often from the Psalms.

"'Lord, thou hast been our dwelling place in all generations,'" he read in a reverent and meaningful voice. Then he would look at Viva, and somehow he knew that she wanted ever to be found in that dwelling place. And in all dwelling places, whether of earth or heaven, he wanted to have her by his side.

One evening, the second week of Viva's stay, she and Jack sat in the usual rockers talking, as they often did, of canvassing life. The fire sent out fitful shafts of light around the draft door. After a while the conversation fell into silence. Then, drawing his chair closer to hers, Jack began to talk softly. "Viva," he said, "since our aim in life is the same, that is to serve our God, don't you think our lives should be united? I do love you, and with a joint love and purpose we could

Into the Blizzard

accomplish much more together." He paused and reached for her hand.

"Next week," he went on, "I have been invited to attend the Union Conference session in Winnipeg. If you come too, we could be married there. What do you say?" And putting his arms around her, he murmured, his lips against her hair, "I do love you, Viva. God has sent you to be my life companion. I know it."

"I know it too," she answered softly, raising a radiant face to his. "I will meet you in Winnipeg," she promised.

The next week Jack went to Winnipeg as planned, and in a few days Viva went to Alex's house in town to meet Helyar and Lenna Zachary.

The Zacharys welcomed her warmly. Jack's mother kissed her and said, "I am so glad my Jacob has at last such a good girl."

"You are welcome, welcome," Father Zachary said, taking both her hands.

Next morning Alex took her to catch the seven-o'clock train to Winnipeg, where Jack was waiting.

Jack and Viva built a solid marriage. Jack never tires of saying, "'Viva' means 'life.' With her I found my life."

Less than two years after their marriage, Jack felt a burden to get back into the colporteur work. He decided to go into northern Alberta. While walking along the rim of a canyon one day he misstepped and found himself falling over a precipice and onto the rocky ground some thirty feet below. He landed on his knees and knew at once that he had broken some bones. Unable to walk, he began painfully to drag himself, floundering along until he reached the road where he was finally picked up and taken to the hospital. There he learned that both kneecaps had been broken. It took a long time for the broken bones to heal, and when he could finally walk again he knew that his days of canvassing were over. He thanked God that he was not crippled, but he knew now he would no longer be able to hike over the trails as he once had.

How could he now tell others about the story of salvation? He would not be able to go door to door.

One day his mother said, "Jacob, why don't you mill flour as my father used to do? There is no such thing as good whole flour to be

168

had these days. I believe people would buy it if they only knew how good it is."

Jack thought seriously about his mother's suggestion. Why, here was an idea. He would mill flour. People would come to him, and he would still be a witness. He ordered the millstones from Germany, and at a much-reduced price secured an abandoned steam boiler. This, repaired with new tubing, became the source of power for the mill. The first flour had a large percentage of ground rock in it because the stones weren't set right, but with a few suggestions from a wise old miller in the vicinity, Jack was able to adjust it, and at last produced his first whole wheat flour. In time he developed a silk screen sifting process which produced the finest of whole wheat flour. Even the most delicate digestion could tolerate it, and it could be made into whole-grain rolls and bread that were light and delicious. The Zachary flour became popular wherever it was sold. But even more important with every sale of flour at his mill, Jack Zachary told the story of salvation.

The Zacharys' five children are now grown and married. Hudson, their only son, is a minister and head of the Bible department at the Mountain View College in the Philippines, while their four daughters, Doreen, Myrtle, Dolores, and Arnetta, are all rearing their families in the fear of the Lord. Jack and Viva now live in a cabin in the mountains near Lytton, British Columbia, and are active in bringing the light they carry to those about them.

Jack has never forgotten the day he learned that God is his Father, a Father who can forgive sin, who can send rain without clouds, and whose emissary he is—a heavenly Father who, just as surely as He has a place prepared for us in heaven, has a place for us to labor for Him on this earth. And one of Jack Zachary's favorite texts is, "Now unto Him that is able to keep you from falling, and to present you faultless before the presence of His glory with exceeding joy, ...be glory and majesty, dominion and power, both now and ever."

We invite you to view the complete
selection of titles we publish at:

www.TEACHServices.com

or write or email us your praises,
reactions, or thoughts about this
or any other book we publish at:

TEACH Services, Inc.
P.O. Box 954
Ringgold, GA 30736

info@TEACHServices.com

CPSIA information can be obtained
at www.ICGtesting.com
Printed in the USA
FFHW021146121218
49757960-54257FF

9 781572 581586